Financial campaigner and self-confessed finance geek, Alice Tapper is the founder and author of Go Fund Yourself, a book, online platform and Instagram account which makes personal finance relevant and relatable.

Online, she has become known for her simple and relatable money guides, and weekly news bulletins which make complex topics, digestible and entertaining.

Alice is the face behind the #regulateBuyNowPayLater campaign which launched in June 2020.

GO FUND YOURSELF®

WHAT MONEY MEANS IN THE 21ST CENTURY,
HOW TO BE GOOD AT IT AND LIVE YOUR BEST LIFE

ALICE TAPPER

HEAD of ZEUS

An Anima Book

This is an Anima book, first published in the UK in 2019 by Head of Zeus Ltd
This Anima paperback first published in 2020 by Head of Zeus Ltd

9 7 5 3 1 2 4 6 8

A catalogue record for this book is available from
the British Library.

ISBN (PB): 9781838931100
ISBN (E): 9781788546713

Diagrams pp. 95, 186, 227 by Sylvie Rabbe
Typeset by Ed Pickford

Printed and bound in Great Britain by
CPI Group (UK) Ltd, Croydon CR0 4YY

Head of Zeus Ltd
5–8 Hardwick Street
London EC1R 4RG
www.headofzeus.com

To my parents

Contents

PART III – START IT

PART IV – SPEND IT

PART 1: HOW WE SPEND IT TODAY

PART 2: THE 'SPENDING' IT ESSENTIALS

PART V – INVEST IT

PART 1: SAVE AND INVEST

Introduction

Hey! Guess what... I got the job!
I've handed in my notice so I'll be starting in 6 weeks.

OMG I knew you would. Congrats!
What's the salary?

I can say, with near certainty, that this conversation has never happened.

It has always struck me that even amongst my closest friends, and let me tell you nothing is off limits, the topic of money is a mood changer. It's rarely discussed as a group, then, every now and again, when one of us has a new job or gets a promotion, someone lets a figure slip or divulges a tiny insight into their financial life. It's not that this is received badly, but it feels like a private disclosure has been made, like you've been let in on a secret. Naturally, learning about someone's earnings leads you to make a comparison of your own – but why is this? How, in a culture of such openness, is money still a no-go subject?

Some have more, some have less, some of us are spenders, others are savers, but whoever you are, and however much you have, money and your relationship with it will play a huge role in your life. At school, we're taught about everything, from tectonic plates to, quite rightly, sex. So how on earth has something so pivotal to adult life slipped through the syllabus and become something that we just have to 'pick up'? I don't see Pythagoras paying my tax bill.

But money doesn't exist in a vacuum. Even if schools had taught us everything you could ever know about pensions and debt, or if we'd been read personal finance books as bedtime stories, this would only have gone so far. Money is always changing. Not only in a functional sense: changing interest rates or the fact that we're quickly moving to a cashless society, but also our relationship with it. How we earn, spend and think about money is evolving.

The economy, politics and technology are the three major forces responsible for casting our money into a state of flux, moulding how we think about our finances and in turn make decisions about them. Since the turn of the century, marked by the bursting of the dot-com bubble, these forces have combined and manifest themselves in unprecedented ways. Nobody is immune to these shifts but, for younger generations growing up in and around the 21st century, there have been unique and magnified effects. We're constrained in ways that previous generations haven't been but have opportunities that our ancestors couldn't have even imagined.

You see, part of the problem with personal finance as it stands is that it tends to centre on what we should do: stop buying coffee, move to Zone 129 and walk to work. Throw in the old generational tropes about avocado toast eating away your house deposit and it's no wonder we're so uninspired to take control of our money. Nobody is motivated by being told what they can't have. Of course, it's not that spending doesn't matter. Budgets are important, but they're not inspirational. The second problem with personal finance is that it's not really personal at all. Yeah, sure, you can learn about the most tax-efficient way to save, but what about the bigger picture – what does money mean in your life? Not just how much you have and how much you spend, but what about the way you earn it, how you think about it and, more to the point, how does it work in our time?

What is this book?

Go Fund Yourself isn't about cutting back on coffee or walking to work and it definitely isn't about becoming a bazillionaire overnight. I don't believe in telling you what you should and shouldn't spend your money on and, sadly, get rich quick schemes are a load of BS. *Go Fund Yourself* is about the bigger picture.

Through the lens of five sections: 'Learn it', 'Earn it', 'Start it', 'Spend it' and 'Invest it', I explore not just how you spend your money but your entire financial life. Because what's the point in trying to save if you don't have a financial dream and what good is a decent paycheque if you loathe every minute spent earning it? We'll look beyond the reductive tales of our generation carelessly frittering away our house deposits, and into the real root of our financial woes, exploring how money works now and what we can do to be good at it. Whilst covering all the essentials that we should have been taught at school, but weren't, each section will investigate the big financial challenges and opportunities we face today – from what the #richkidsofinstagram have to do with you and your money, why spending no longer means owning, how consumerism is changing our financial mindsets and how being open about our finances could make us all richer.

Rather than focusing on the small tweaks (although we'll cover those too), this book will shed light on the big changes and choices that really make a difference to your life. From how to set up a system to get you out of debt faster, to how to earn money doing something you love and take steps towards validating and starting a business. This isn't a new-fangled programme or scheme with an unrealistic promise of setting you up for retirement before forty. In fact, most of the advice contained in this book isn't new at all. I've simply drawn on my own experience and packaged up the tried, tested and trusted techniques across a range of topics and interwoven them with stories about how money works today. But most importantly, this book is about you and your life. I'm not going to make any assumptions about what you do and don't spend your money on, or judgements about how you spend it. Instead, I'll help you identify what your best financial life looks like and show you how to get there. Basically, I've written the book that I've always wished existed.

Who is this book for?

By virtue of the fact that I am myself a twenty-something, and because the book looks specifically at the opportunities and challenges facing younger generations today, it probably speaks more to a twenty- or thirty-something crowd. Of course, there might be themes and trends you don't agree with or that aren't relevant to you and that's cool. Just take what's useful and leave what isn't. I'm not a fan of generational labels such as 'Millennial' and 'Gen Z' but I did need some vocab to broadly describe you, my target audience, so I set on speaking about 'younger generations' or 'our generation'. All this being said, most of the practical advice contained within the book is age-neutral and I hope that it might be useful to anyone of any age.

Time isn't money

I'm sure Benjamin Franklin meant well when, in his book *Advice to a Young Tradesman*, he suggested that 'Time is Money'. It's a principle that forms the cornerstone of the entire labour market. Just look at any employment contract that will detail exactly how many hours per week you'll work for X amount of cash. We even talk about time in financial terms: 'spending', 'saving' and 'buying' it, as if it were a tradable commodity or something that can be withdrawn from an ATM. What you do with your time does affect how much money you make; spend it well and time can *make* money, just as spending it poorly can see it wasted. However, to say time *is* money implies that somehow they are of equal value or that our time has a price. The reality is, time isn't an asset in the same way that money is. Whilst we kid ourselves into thinking that it's spendable, buyable and saveable, it's just not. Although money can create opportunities to spend your time differently, you can't get more of it and most of us don't really know how much of it we have to spend. What we do know is that, in the economy of time, you're only ever getting poorer. Sorry, I know most personal finance books don't usually get so existential, but it's up from here, I promise.

Understanding the difference between time and money is one of the most significant shifts we can make in our financial and working lives. When we choose to see time as infinitely valuable, we treat it like it is. We make better decisions about our time, and also better decisions about our money and how we earn it. Rather than putting a price on our precious hours we choose to do things with them, not because someone is paying you enough to justify the sacrifice, but because you actually want to. You spend time because it's an investment that returns more than just cash in the bank.

Changing our perspective on money and time also shifts our thinking around how we earn it and what we do with it. Typically we see earning as a one-dimensional thing – you put in the hours (and the rest…) and then get paid.

THREE TYPES OF INCOME

ACTIVE

Money made from exchanging your time for money:

SALARY, WAGES, BONUS, COMMISSION, CONSULTING/ SERVICES

PASSIVE

Money made from assets you have purchased or created:

BUSINESS, ROYALTIES, PROPERTY (RENT)

PORTFOLIO

Money made by selling an investment at a higher price than you paid for it:

INVESTMENTS, DIVIDENDS, INTEREST, CAPITAL GAINS

But if you take away anything from this book, I hope it's that money is so much more than something you earn and spend; that's just one teeny corner in an entire universe that is money.

For example, in 'Earn it', we'll look at active income: getting to the bottom of how to earn money in ways that are worth your precious time whilst exploring the best strategies to make the career changes and choices that'll get you living your best working life. In 'Invest it', we'll focus on portfolio income: lifting the lid on the elusive world of the stock market, teaching you the secrets to getting rich slowly and why being young is your greatest asset. 'Start it' will focus on passive income: for anyone who has ever thought about starting a business, this chapter will start with the basics of business ideas, how to validate them and manage the financials of being an entrepreneur.

A disclaimer

Whilst there are many things that I hope this book will give you, one thing that it can't do is offer personalized financial, legal, tax or other advice of any kind. Instead, it offers the time-tested but generic advice and information that will help you get good at money and feel better about it. When it comes to investing, remember that your capital (the money you invest) is at risk. The value of your investments can go down as well as up and you may get back less than you invest. If you need advice on your specific circumstances, you should speak to an independent financial advisor.

Before you spend your hard-earned dollar on this book it's probably worth noting what this book isn't. It definitely isn't intended to be a 'guide on everything you could ever need to know about personal finance'. I have included specific detail that I think will be useful to most people, but for further information I'd recommend the plethora of personal finance websites that house all the nitty-gritty detail your heart could desire. Cue god of personal finance, Martin Lewis.

Another thing this book isn't is a quantum-theoretical approach to money, income and time (I'm not sure what that is, but it does exist if that's what you're after). I'm definitely not an academic and it isn't going to talk you through the intricacies of hedging, call options and derivatives (we can all breathe a sigh of relief).

The GFY Money Plan

Although I recommend you read the book as a whole, I know that whilst it's all very well knowing what to do, knowing when to do it can be a total minefield. Whilst thinking about how I could overcome this problem, I came up with the idea of a step by step guide to the seven most important steps you can take to live your best financial life. Meet the GFY Money Plan. Remember that this isn't financial advice; it's a guide which contains personal finance 'rules of thumb', but at the end of the day, do what feels right for you.

Step 1: You've got goals

> Sort your money mindset (pp. 148–51)
> Define your ideal income (pp. 55–6)

Forget #couplegoals, let's talk #moneygoals. Rather than jumping into the 'whats' and 'hows' of money management, what about the why? Why did you buy this book? Apart from the obvious ambitions of wanting more cash in the bank, what do you really want?

Maybe you're thinking about saving for a deposit on a house or planning a blow-out trip around the world. Or are you currently head in sand and in need of some encouragement to just take a little peek at your finances? Maybe you're earning decent money but in a job that just isn't worth the dollar? Whatever your dreams or worries, it's important to know what they are. This will keep you focused but it also helps you work out what you should be doing with your money today, the kind of investments you should make and the risks you should be willing to take.

So what do you want to achieve? What does your best financial life look like?

Think about your goals, short, medium and long term, and work out a realistic timeframe for you to achieve them in. If you don't know what they are yet, that's OK. Come back to this later. This book will help you sort them out.

- **Short** (1 year) e.g. Negotiate a payrise
- **Medium** (1–5 years) e.g. Pay off all debts
- **Long term** (5+ years) e.g. Save enough of a deposit to buy a £400,000 flat

Step 2: You've got an emergency fund

> Budget better, spend better (pp. 152–60)

Fun, fun, fu**. Nasty (and expensive) surprises can come out of nowhere so make sure you've got some savings to provide you with some financial cushioning for those 'in emergency break glass' situations. The exact amount that you need to save will depend on your own circumstances. £1,000 is often thrown around as a suggested figure but it's not one-size-fits-all. Think about your own lifestyle, responsibilities and security.

For instance someone with a four-bedroom house and three kids will probably want a bigger buffer than a single twenty-something living with their parents. To calculate your own, get negative. Think about all the things that could possibly go wrong financially and how much it might cost you to put them right. For help, go to p. 55 where you can define your financial needs.

Having an emergency fund will not only carry you through financially dark times of job loss or medical emergencies, but it can be an empowering thing too. In 2016 Paulette Perhach's viral article 'A Story of a Fuck Off Fund' gave a 'sliding door' style account of a woman faced with both an abusive boss and boyfriend. In reality, without savings, she is trapped, powerless and in the grip of her abusers. In her alternate world, however, her nest-egg gives her the freedom and independence to walk away from the misery and onto something better. Money really is power.

Step 3: You've paid off expensive debts

> Understand good vs bad debt (pp. 162–3)
> The GFY get out of debt plan (pp. 164–9)

The majority of younger generations are no stranger to debt. Be it student loans, overdrafts or credit cards. In the UK we have an average total debt per household of £59,409, paying £1,886 per year on interest repayments alone. However, not all debt is equal. Before investing, prioritize paying off debts with high interest rates and expensive fees i.e. bad debts. This can be a completely overwhelming task, so for a plan on how to make getting out of debt simpler use the GFY get out of debt plan.

Step 4: You've got a pension and have maximized contributions

> Investing in your retirement for the self-employed (pp. 198–9)

Pension, sch-mension. Yes, your eyes may roll at the very mention of 'retirement' but having a pension is one of the easiest and most important ways to create wealth and prepare for the future. Pension contributions are basically a way to protect a proportion of your income from tax, invest it and save it for later life. This benefit is called 'tax relief'. Say you are a basic-rate taxpayer and contribute £100 from your salary into your pension, it would actually only cost you £80. The government adds the extra £20 on top – what it would have taken in tax from £100 of your salary. Pensions are invested in stocks and shares but typically you'll have a pension provider who takes care of all that for you. Having a pension plus money to invest in the stock market gives you the best of both worlds.

There are three types of pension that you should know about:

- **Workplace pension** – All employers are legally obliged to provide a pension to employees with one of the perks being that your employer will often match your contributions up to a certain percentage of your salary.

If this is the case, it's worth checking with your HR department to ensure that you are contributing the maximum amount you can afford in order to make the most of your employer's contributions

- **Personal pension** – This is the one that you set up with a pension provider, independent of your employer. In this instance, you choose your contributions. Personal pensions are a useful solution if you're self-employed or if you feel your workplace pension isn't enough. There are two main types of personal pension: stakeholder pensions, which have low and flexible minimum contributions and a default investment strategy, and self-invested personal pensions (SIPP), where you choose your own investments

- **State pension** – In the UK, the government provides regular pension payments to any National Insurance payer of pension age (currently mid-sixties but this is due to increase to sixty-seven by 2028). You don't want to have to solely rely on a state pension (it's £8,767.20 per year at the moment) so make sure you maximize your workplace pension or set up a personal pension

Step 5: Boost your emergency fund

❯ Budget better, spend better (pp. 152–60)

If you've paid off your bad debt and sorted out your pension, then you will have already completed Step 2, which is starting an emergency fund. Step 5 is simply boosting your emergency fund so you've got a decent savings pot. The amount you need to stash away will depend on your own circumstances and living costs but at least three months' worth of living expenses is about right. For those in unstable employment or if you're a freelancer, you might want to save more. If three months seems completely overwhelming, work out how much, if the worst came to the worst, you could realistically live off. How could you scale back on your living costs? Use p. 55 to help define your financial needs.

Step 6: Start investing

> Investing if your goals are more than five years away
> (p. 198)

> Investing if your goals are less than five years away
> (p. 198)

In theory, you are now at liberty to throw your money at the markets with the exuberance of Jordan Belfort, but before you do – please read 'Invest it' (pp. 179–238).

Heed the wisdom of Warren Buffett: 'I never invest in anything that I don't understand.' It sounds obvious but history reveals a pattern of investors chucking money at investments that they simply don't get. The 2008 global banking crisis was a perfect example; billions of dollars had been invested in sub-prime mortgage backed securities: investment packages full of mortgages that ultimately people would never pay back. Whatever you choose to invest in (we'll get to the methods in Part V), it's important that you know a bit about how the stock market operates as a whole and what drives the value of your investments. You also want to make sure you've got a handle on the day-to-day running of your own finances. This means understanding what's coming in, going out and what you're able to add to your investment pot each month. When it comes to investing, you should be looking to invest for at least five years, meaning you're in the market long enough to make losing money less likely.

If your goals are less than five years away, you can still consider 'investing', however, you probably won't want to invest in shares. More about this on p. 198.

Step 7: Live and give

> Live and give (p. 238)

I didn't call this book *Go Fund Yourself: What money means in the 21st century, how to be good at it and have as much as possible*. That's not what this book is about. Instead, this book is about earning, spending and investing your money in a way that helps you love your life and maybe helps other people love theirs a bit more too.

PART I

LEARN IT

Money is...

The banks and you

Interest rates

How to lose money by doing nothing

Money is...

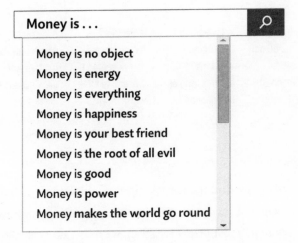

Money is **no object**
Money is **energy**
Money is **everything**
Money is **happiness**
Money is **your best friend**
Money is **the root of all evil**
Money is **good**
Money is **power**
Money **makes the world go round**

Leave aside the various philosophical questions as to what money is (more on those later); let's first look at what it is in practical terms. How has money as we know it today come into existence? And what's the future?

Throughout the ages money has evolved, but, at its core, it has always done the same job: it's a means of 'exchange'. In its earliest form, this didn't involve physical money at all; the barter system allowed people to swap their goods and services for other people's goods and services. You can imagine how restrictive this could be: you try bartering with your local barista for your flat white every morning.

COMMODITY MONEY	REPRESENTATIVE MONEY	FIAT MONEY	CRYPTOCURRENCY
Has intrinsic value based on the material from which it's made.	Is backed by something of value e.g. gold, but has little or no value of its own.	Is declared by the government and accepted by citizens to have worth.	A currency which only exists digitally and uses advanced encryption techniques for security.

In 1100 BC we find the earliest signs of objects being used as a store of value or medium of exchange. Commodity money was currency in its most primitive form, with its value based on the material it was made from. The thinking goes that some time around 1100 BC, the Chinese moved from using actual tools and weapons as a medium of exchange to miniature replicas of the same tools cast in bronze. For convenience, the tiny weapons were eventually abandoned in favour of round tokens, giving rise to the much-improved medium of exchange: the coin. Around the world there were examples of all sorts of objects being used as currency. Gold and silver were perhaps the most commonly used but other items, including cowrie shells, were used widely across much of Africa and Asia.

The florin of AD 1250 was the first gold coin to be widely accepted across Europe which created significant advancements in international trade; but, as you might imagine, lugging around a bag of gold coins was neither convenient nor safe. So, by the 1700s, banknotes had become commonplace: a way of depositing your precious metals in exchange for a promissory note. This is known as 'representative money': while the money itself isn't of value, it's backed by something that is (e.g. gold or silver). To this day, British notes are still marked with the emblem: 'I promise to pay the bearer on demand the sum of...'

Today, however, most financial systems are based on 'fiat currency': like representative money, this is without physical value, but it is backed specifically by a government rather than a commodity like silver or gold. Unlike ye olde gold coins, fiat currencies are, in fact, worthless. It's only because we trust the government's declaration that we can all agree on its value. The reason that we perceive a £5 note to be worth £5 is because the government has declared it so.

The banks and you

Like it or not, we do live in a largely capitalist society in which the banks take centre stage.

But what exactly do we mean by a 'bank' and what do they do? As a broad definition, a bank is a financial institution licensed to receive deposits and make loans, but there are three types you should know about.

- **Commercial bank** – Probably the one you are most familiar with. Commercial banks serve small businesses and individuals like you and me. They help keep our money secure, receive deposits and also make short- and long-term loans, which include financial products such as mortgages. Traditionally these were found on the high street, but in recent years, new-age digital commercial banks have emerged, with no physical presence
- **Investment bank** – Like a commercial bank, only their customers are large corporate organizations. Following the 2008 financial crisis, investment banks received a bad rap (and some even collapsed) due to the role they played in the creation and trading of dubious financial products
- **Central bank** – Unlike commercial and investment banks, a central bank serves an entire state, managing their currency, money supply and interest rates. They have a unique authority in being able to print more of a currency, which is known as 'quantitative easing', and can act as the 'lender of last resort' to investment and commercial banks, meaning they are able to bail them out in a financial crisis. The role of the central bank is to ensure the financial and monetary health of the economy, much of which involves managing and promoting healthy economic growth

Economic growth – an increase in the production of goods and services over a specific period

GDP (Gross Domestic Product) – the most commonly used measure of a country's economic health. It adds up all goods and services that a country produces within a specific period

Real GDP – The measure of GDP which removes the effects of inflation (defined on the next page). This makes it a more accurate measure of how an economy is growing

Interest rates

When we talk about a 'bank' most of us are referring to commercial banks: the ones which hold our personal savings and debts. But it is the central bank that has the most influence over the flow of money in the economy: it governs interest rate levels and controls the supply of currency. Think of these factors as two dials that the central bank can turn up or down depending on the state of the economy.

Interest – What you pay for borrowing money, and what banks pay to you for saving money

How do interest rates work?

Typically, when the central bank wants to give the economy a little nudge and increase levels of consumer spending, it will lower interest rates. The thinking behind doing this is that it reduces the incentive to squirrel away our savings in a bank account and makes us more likely to spend, spend, spend! However, economic growth often comes with inflation.

Inflation – A rise in prices that causes a rise in the cost of living

When the central bank wants to curb inflation, it will raise interest rates. When interest rates are higher, saving sounds like a much better deal, so rather than spend, we're more likely to lock away our savings. This, in turn, takes the pressure off rising prices.

When an increase or decrease in the interest rates is talked about in the news, this is referring to the 'Bank Rate', which in the UK is set by the Bank of England's (the UK's central bank) Monetary Policy Committee (MPC), chaired by the Governor of the Bank of England, eight times a year. The Bank Rate is the rate that the Bank of England pays commercial banks for holding money with them (known as 'reserves') and is usually passed on to you and me. The rate set by commercial banks affects both the amount it costs to borrow money and the amount we get for saving it.

However, I'm sure you'll have noticed that commercial banks don't all offer the same interest rates and will often promise higher returns. When you borrow money, banks will vary the rate depending on the amount of risk they are taking on. For example, they'll consider the value of the loan and your track record in paying off debts. In the case of savings accounts, where a bank is promising you some interest in return for keeping your money with them, interest rates will depend on a number of factors such as the amount you are investing and the length of time you're willing to keep your hands off it. So, this all sounds pretty good, right? Tuck your money up in a high-interest account and watch the money roll in? Right? Sadly not. Have a browse through the 'savings account' section on the website of any commercial bank and those dreams of an early retirement in the Maldives will quickly be dampened. At the very most, you're probably looking at no more than 1.75 per cent AER (Annual Equivalent Rate). So, say you're wanting to save £1,000, this means by the end of the year you will have earned £17.50 on your savings.

How to lose money by doing nothing

Remember when Freddos were 10p and cinema tickets were less than a fiver? Damn we had it so good. Whilst inflation is a sign of economic growth, it can spell plummeting disposable income if wages don't keep up. When prices rise faster than your pay, then the amount of money you have to spend goes down in real terms.

The second way that inflation dents your personal finances is in the deceptively 'secure' confines of your savings account. Let's say you have £100 in a savings account that pays you a 1 per cent interest rate. After a year, you will have £101 in your account. However, if inflation runs at 2 per cent (i.e. prices have risen by this much, on average), you would need to have £102 to make up for the impact of higher prices. So, in effect, you're £1 worse off in terms of your purchasing power. One pound might seem neither here nor there, but, over the years, the accumulated effect of inflation will munch away at your hard-earned cash. The good news is, unlike your stagnant wages, you can do something to protect your savings, which we'll get to in Part V – 'Invest it'.

PART II

EARN IT

A brief history of 'earning it'

Digital natives

Generation squeeze

PART 1: MAKING CHOICES

Overload

Expectations and access

How to make decisions

PART 2: MAKING CHANGES

Get the basics right

Big changes

A brief history of 'earning it'

How we earn money is always evolving but the Industrial Revolution saw the first major turning point. After ground-breaking innovations in artificial lighting and steam power, new and exciting opportunities emerged. Unlike before, when workers had been limited to unstable and poorly paid seasonal farm work, cities offered a promising future, albeit without the rights, health and safety laws, and HR departments that today we take for granted. Factory workers had no choice but to work up to eighteen-hour days and in pretty rough conditions. It wasn't long before unions helped to give workers protection laws and a cap on working hours, renewing economic growth and driving technological development. With the introduction of workers' rights came a gradual fall in working hours throughout the 20th century. In the US and UK, we settled at a comfortable eight-hour day, five-day week, giving rise to the familiar '9–5'. Of course, for many, the idea of an actual 9–5 is the stuff of dreams. Whilst most employment contracts will optimistically cite a thirty-five to forty-hour week and promise a one-hour lunchbreak, hopes are often dashed when workplace reality hits and we find ourselves tucking into a lunchtime meal deal at our desk and cancelling dinner plans in favour of an evening in with Microsoft PowerPoint.

Because what we actually mean by 9–5 isn't a shorthand for the number of hours we typically work in a day. It has evolved into something more. It connotes employment of stability, predictability and low risk. In other words, a good job, at a big company, that pays well. These are the markers of success and privilege that workers fought hard for in the wake of the Industrial Revolution.

However, the first world is seeing giant shifts in what it means to be employed. The way we work today would be barely recognizable to an 18th-century trade unionist.

For some, the predictability and stability of the traditional 9–5 has, to some extent, lost its appeal. We're seeing start-ups snapping at the heels of lumbering corporates which have neglected to improve the work-life experience and twenty-somethings jacking in the day job to go freelance or do their own thing. And what even is a 'job' anyway? For others, the security that was once fought hard for is becoming an impossibility, with zero-hour contracts and the gig economy reshaping the entire employee–employer relationship.

So how has this happened? How come there is disconnect between the demands of employers and desires of employees?

Why is safe and secure employment no longer enough for some?

A common response is to blame 'the youth of today' for being fundamentally incapable of the hard graft that serious careers might demand. We're far too busy finding a table for brunch or perfecting Instagram captions to be planning our career strategy. But look to the root of these shifts and you'll find they have very little to do with our breakfast preferences or penchant for plant-based diets. They are, instead, largely symptoms of the changing economic and technological climate of the last twenty years. It just so happens that it's younger generations who are feeling the consequences of these shifts the most.

Digital natives

'See you on MSN, yeah?' The words of every nineties teen as the school day ended. If you were born after 1996, you probably have no idea what I'm on about, testament alone to how quickly things change. It's impossible to ignore the enormous role that technology is playing in shaping our opportunities, ambitions and sense of self. If you're under the age of thirty-five you're a digital native, and have either witnessed the proliferation of the internet during your childhood or have never known a world without it. We're familiar with a handful of negative truths about its impact on our lives; the fact that it's in part responsible for the increasing disconnection and loneliness in society and its role in cultivating unhelpful and unrealistic norms around what the perfect body looks like. But what about our changing attitudes to how we earn money?

When Facebook was founded, Mark Zuckerberg described it as a 'social network'; a platform that would leverage the power of the internet to connect college students. But, in a short space of time, it and the handful of other social platforms have evolved into entirely different beasts. We're living in an age where our social lives have been duplicated, existing both offline and online, and where 'connection' has been reduced to a quick double tap on a shiny screen.

The original purpose of these sites is now very much secondary. It's no coincidence that the terminology, 'social network', implying a two-way connection, has slipped from our vocabularies, replaced instead by 'media', a term much less about connection and much more about self-projection.

I was generation Bebo: an infantile Facebook that allowed you to rank your best friends, build quizzes to see which of your school mates *really* knew you, and write a mini-biography under a section called 'Me, Myself and I'. Who knows where the allegations of 'generation narcissist' were born?! For kids emerging into an era where their parents had yet to be inaugurated as members of the world wide web, social media existed as a digital playground and we were let loose to curate and shape our own online identity. Kids tend to be the early adopters; the first to conquer the ground of the internet landscape, staking their claim before moving on to newer, cooler pastures. A prime example is Facebook, which was initially used by eighteen- to twenty-year-old college students, and has since seen an exodus of its younger users with the average age rising rapidly in recent years.

Individualism and the importance we place on 'the self' has bled over into real life too. Whilst our twenties have always been a decade of freedom from responsibility, the postponing of big life decisions such as marriage and kids has given us even more time to cultivate ourselves. According to the Global Wellness Economy Monitor, 'wellness-tourism' is now a $563 billion industry, growing at a faster rate than the tourism industry itself.

The 'self-care' movement has seen 'treating yo-self' transformed into a reverential experience, perhaps even obligation, and is documented (of course) in over 13 million Instagram photos (#selfcare). And now, consumer tech is changing the way our own needs are met. Bending to meet our wants and whims is a realm of services served up on a touchscreen platter and delivered at exactly the right time and in perfect proportion. Massages on demand, a late-night pizza (sourdough of course) with *vegan* cheese and a taxi with precisely the right number of seats to ship you and the entourage to Friday night's destination. Cue the Backstreet Boys: 'I want it that way…'

We're living in a time where we, as individuals, have never had so much power. A few years back and celeb-dom was limited to the confines of TV and film. Sure, there might have been the odd celebrity endorsement, but the weight of influence lay in the hands of well-established high street institutions. Social media has turned the brand–consumer dynamic on its head, shifting the commercial power from billion-pound corporations to an army of 'Influencers' with the ability to reach the same number of eyes with a single Instagram post as a multi-million-pound TV commercial. At the frontier of this new era of influence is, without doubt, the Kardashian–Jenner clan; digital-queens with a natural gift for translating drama to influence, and influence to money. In 2018, Kylie Jenner, aged twenty, was revealed to be worth a staggering $900 million (£680 million); a fortune largely gained through her lip-kit business, which has put her on track to become the world's youngest self-made billionaire. So not only are we existing in an age where our sense of self and individuality is held in such high regard, but the 'power potential' of a single individual has never been greater.

Now contrast all of this with your average workplace. There is a disconnect; to this day, many large companies still hold on to archaic protocols: numbering their employees and conducting anonymous annual reviews. With research finding that we're defining ourselves less by our work and more so by our friends, family and what we do outside of the office, it's no wonder that we're moving from job to job at an ever-quickening rate. For big companies that previously retained their employees with air miles, prestigious brand names and swanky offices, this is a problem that isn't going away. It makes sense that when plunged into a corporate life with a steep hierarchy, bureaucratic process and where the weight of opinion is heavily skewed to senior employees, that disillusionment sets in. The sense of individuality and freedom that we've grown so used to isn't translating well.

To add to this frustration, we know that more is possible. It's not that dreaming of purpose and impact is a new phenomenon that is unique to our time. Be it freedom, independence or purpose, for some, there has always been a drive to find a job that you want to get out of bed for or a means to generate your own income and provide for ourselves and escape the 9–5 (cue Dolly Parton).

Now, the difference is, it's never been more achievable. We know that technology can create more efficient, flexible ways of working and that flatter organizational structures can increase motivation. Social media and the internet more broadly have both created new kinds of opportunity and connected us to the stories of people who are pursuing them, be it the Zuckerbergs and Bezoses who have created billion-dollar companies or creative entrepreneurs forging online careers from their bedrooms. We know that more is possible and many of us want a piece of it.

Generation squeeze

The economic experience of the past twenty years has also created huge shifts in how we perceive work and make decisions around earning money. Every generation has its own struggles, but in terms of the personal finances of those born between 1981 and 2000 things aren't looking great. The financial crisis of 2008 has contributed to a financial hangover, lingering mostly amongst younger generations. There is some good news: those born between 1981 and 2000 are experiencing 25 per cent lower unemployment than baby boomers (born 1946–65) at the same age. However, whilst we're more likely to be working, the rewards for doing so have diminished. In the six years between the start of 2009 and the end of 2014, pay growth failed to keep up with inflation, creating a pay-squeeze that has since returned in 2017 following the Brexit referendum. Adjusting for inflation, average pay in 2018 was still £15 a week below the pre-2008 levels, with those born between 1981 and 2000 earning the same that those born between 1966 and 1980 were earning at the same age. Historically, wages, disposable income and, in turn, living standards have risen generation on generation, but for the 1981–2000 cohort there has been no progress.

And so what? We still have high living standards, even if we're not richer than generations previous. What's the problem? Well, there's a huge one. Whilst wages remained at uninspiring lows, property prices and rents have climbed to eye-watering highs. Throw in some inflation and tightened mortgage regulations for good measure and you're looking at a generation where one-third will be renting for their entire lives, and the average thirty-year-old will have spent £44,000 more on rent than the average baby boomer of the same age.

It's little wonder that attitudes to work have changed, with the most recent entrants to the workforce suffering from plummeting levels of job satisfaction. It's not all about high expectations or narcissistic tendencies. It's that today's expectations and motivations are different. In a world where the income you earn might only just cover your basic living costs, and afford you fewer opportunities to splash your cash, you sure as hell want to be enjoying the time spent earning it. We want money. Of course. We *need* money. But we also want work to be more than just a transactional exchange of 'my time for your cash'. Because whilst companies may bleat on about 'work–life balance' and 'flexible working', at the end of the day, work is life. We spend 50 per cent of our waking hours doing it, so if you're not living then when are you?

In between our ever-tightening income and the bleak media headlines, there is a call to action: to consider more carefully how we spend our time and earn our money. The media's favourite generational tropes aren't going away soon and whilst wages have begun to resurrect, there is still some major catching up to do. So, what can *you* do? How can you be more fulfilled in your working life and earn money in a way that not only pays the bills but aligns with your own values and identity? In the next part of this chapter we'll look at exactly that.

PART 1: MAKING CHOICES

There are those infuriatingly 'together' people who have always known what they've wanted to do with their lives, and then there are people like me. The issue wasn't that I didn't know what I wanted to be, it's that I wanted to be it ALL.

Whilst we really do have the potential to do a variety of different jobs and whilst it's perfectly possible to change careers later on (more on that soon), sadly it's just not possible to be a doctor, football agent *and* a turtle conservationist all at once. This means waving goodbye to and possibly even mourning the many other lives that might have been.

But before we even get to this stage, decisions must be made. Whilst, in principle, options are a great thing, for some (me) decisions, particularly life changing ones, are a nightmare.

There's a tendency to imagine your career like this: a straightforward path on which you plod from education to work, and work through to retirement. There might be forks along the way: important decisions that'll impact your journey and also the destination. And for those who know exactly which path they want to follow and where they want to 'end up', this kind of visualization makes total sense.

The problem arises for people like me. When you're not sure what you want to 'be' the idea of mapping out your entire career trajectory seems completely terrifying. In the final few months of university, seemingly the only person without a five-year plan and a back catalogue of prestigious internships, I'd try to imagine what my future life might look like.

It was like standing before an enormous mountain range: me at the foot, faced with thousands of trails that would weave their way to dramatically different destinations. I'd examine the intricacies of all these possible lives. What would I enjoy? Does that sound impressive? Would that make enough money?

This would go on. Not really wanting to really commit to anything for fear that I would make the wrong choice. Whilst making a decision means getting just that little bit closer to doing something, it means waving goodbye to a thousand other lives that might have been. It can feel like any decision you make, no matter how small, will have a decisive impact on your life.

Overload

What makes deciding even harder is the sheer volume of choice we now have.

Technological, environmental and social change is happening at breakneck speed, and with it our needs as consumers. As businesses start up and evolve to meet our changing lifestyles, new jobs are created, jobs that didn't even exist ten years ago. Cast your eye over any job site and you'll find an array of titles better placed in a work of dystopian fiction. 'Chief Listening Officer', 'User Experience Designer', 'Cloud Computing Expert' and 'Sustainability Advisor' are all plausible career choices.

And it's not just careers. Technology tells us we deserve choice; in fact, as a generation, we've come to expect it. From inexhaustible dating apps, more likely to give you a swipe-induced repetitive strain injury before you find the love of your life, to search engines, serving up an infinite source of information for us to peruse. On a daily basis we're faced with both more decisions to be made and more options to choose from.

And, instinctively, choice feels good, right? Particularly for the autonomy-seeking person who values their individuality. It represents freedom and self-determination, all things that we've been encouraged to value. However, could it be that this choice overload actually hinders rather than helps us when it comes to finding fulfilment in our work? Over to you, social scientists...

In one experiment, Barry Schwartz, author of *The Paradox of Choice: Why More Is Less*, set up two displays of preserved goods at a gourmet food store, giving customers the chance to try samples and use a dollar-off coupon if they bought a jar. In one display there were six jams and in the other twenty-four. Whilst we might imagine that variety made for a positive consumer experience, it actually had a negative effect on sales, with 30 per cent of people exposed to the smaller selection buying a jam, as opposed to 3 per cent when shown a larger selection. There's a paradox of choice at play. More worryingly, the research also found that variety makes us more dissatisfied and less content with the choices we end up making, meaning we're mistakenly confusing choice with better outcomes.

Translate these findings to the working world, and it's no wonder we're so at sea: too much choice is making life decisions harder, and the plethora of weird and wonderful career options has raised our expectations to an all-time high. We've come to expect that the perfect career exists for us, when in reality we're more prone to disappointment and regret than ever before.

Expectations and access

Alongside technological change, societal shifts have also begun to ripple their way across the working landscape. For women in particular, we are to some extent less constrained by the demographic factors that would have once held us back. There is still way to go, but fifty years ago a woman with a professional career was an anomaly, now it is a given. This expansion of possibility brings with it the realization that the world really is our oyster, but, perhaps, also heightened pressure to 'achieve'. Whilst we can go further than before, there is more opportunity for failure.

However, whilst in principle career possibilities have never been greater, this doesn't always translate into access. In a 2017 government assessment on social mobility, it was found that the quality of jobs available for young people had actually worsened over the last twenty years. We're more likely to be in involuntary part-time or temporary work, with even graduates suffering: those leaving university have a 10 per cent higher chance of ending up in a non-graduate role for which they were overqualified. The employment options for disadvantaged young people have fared particularly badly, not helped by austerity cuts to careers advice. Without helpful family contacts, there remains little formal support and guidance, widening the knowledge and confidence gap between the advantaged and disadvantaged. Social and economic barriers are ever present. Fact. If you don't have the family contacts at your disposal or the city flat which enables you to take unpaid internships, it's harder, but believing that you can, and that you deserve access to the opportunities afforded by privilege, is vital. It's not easy or fair, but you have to give yourself permission to go after what you want.

Tips to build a career without a 'leg up'

- Build your own network – Search for local networking meetings and relevant events
- Get creative – Use your creativity to stand out. Don't be afraid to catch employers' attention. Tell stories and show them how you are different
- Be specific – Don't just ask if you can 'pick their brains' over coffee. They'll get a million of those requests. Instead think specifically about what it is you want help with and, even better, how you might be able to help them out
- Flatter – Everyone loves a compliment. When reaching out to someone you don't know, personalize your message with a compliment specific to their work
- Cold call – Be brave and just do it. What's the worst that can happen?
- Be smart about who you contact – Once you've identified the companies you admire, think strategically about how to get in touch. The CEO might be a stretch, so do some

digging and find junior employees who could help you out

- Be a bit sneaky – Can't find their email? Once you know the company's domain name (e.g. mine is 'gofundyourself.co') you can use trial and error to work out the rest (it's Alice…)
- Find a mentor – If you're still in education this could be a school teacher, otherwise look at joining a formal mentoring programme that pairs you up with someone in industry

How to make decisions

In any moment of decision, the best thing you can do is the right thing, the next best thing is the wrong thing, and the worst thing you can do is nothing.

Theodore Roosevelt

'What job do you want to do?' The premise of traditional careers advice assumes that we not only understand the intricacies of the entire job market (not to mention how it will change in years to come) but that we also understand ourselves. Unfortunately, the former is impossible and we're pretty terrible at the latter. Knowing what would make a cool job or one that we'll feel proud to tell people we do is easy, but what's hard is knowing and, more to the point, picking a job that we'll actually enjoy doing. Having motivation is essential for success, but being motivated isn't a something that you either have or you don't.

Motivation is the feeling you get back when you direct your energy and time at something you care about and actually want. It's when you stop clock watching and when work doesn't feel like work. Like a relationship, you can't fight for something that just isn't your vibe. When the going gets tough, when your cool new job is no longer new and cool, it'll be near impossible to stick at it long term.

So how do we navigate a world of limitless choice and furiously high expectations? How do we make better decisions to build a working life that not only sounds good over dinner but earns money and ultimately makes us happy?

Step 1: Check your sources

Decisions require information, which means bad information leads to bad decisions. Growing up, we find ourselves absorbing all sorts of data about the world of work, such as which jobs are more prestigious than others, the sort of work that pays well and careers that require an education. We also learn about 'success' and what it means from those around us. So whether your parents enjoyed their jobs will have undoubtedly shaped your own perception of the kind of work you want to do. You might have been inspired by someone older whose work you thought was cool or put off from certain jobs after seeing a family member loathe theirs. This information is useful; it helps us to build a model of success, understand the opportunities out there and learn from those with more experience than us.

However, when making decisions about what to do with our own lives, there's a much more important and unbiased source that is often overlooked: ourselves. It sounds blindingly obvious, but our decisions around careers, particularly mistakes, can so often be tracked back not to ourselves but to the expectations and pressures of the world we live in. When a palliative care nurse listened to her patients' biggest regrets, 'living a life that others expected as opposed to one that was true to themselves' was mentioned most often. Whether it's fame, wealth or a glossy corporate title, our idea of success tends to skew towards what society says we should want, over and above our own vision for our lives. Of course, there is nothing wrong with wanting any of these things, but good decisions tend to be informed by our own knowledge of what we're like, rather than external information that we adopt as truth.

Unfortunately, the education system just isn't set up for this kind of self-discovery. Understandably, school and university curriculums are focused on preparing students for the working world, which makes it so easy to follow the path of least resistance. Maybe you showed a natural talent for the sciences, so it made sense to pick those subjects. Before you know it, you've graduated with a degree in microbiology, when what you really want to be is a graphic designer.

Just as schools are measured on grades, universities are ranked on employment outcomes, not lifetime job satisfaction. They're brilliant at working out what we could do with our lives but not so great at helping us to understand what we really WANT to do. It's a subtle but important distinction that could be the difference between forty years of the Sunday blues and actually loving your job!

We have two options. Either we make choices based on what other people think according to their model of success. Or we write our own rules and build our own model, underpinned by our understanding of who we are, and our skills, strengths and interests. It's only in understanding what *you* want that you can chase it with all the ambition and determination that you have. Because whilst it's miserable to not get what you want, it's even more so if, when it's all over, you discover that what you've been chasing isn't what you wanted after all.

Step 2: Who are you?

Somewhere, in the deep waters between Taiwan and Japan, exists a string of islands called Okinawa. Aside from its crystal blue sea, subtropical climate and sandy beaches, something else has drawn attention to Okinawa. Not the island itself, but its inhabitants, who have become renowned for having one of the world's highest life expectancies, with more than 400 centenarians occupying the island.

So, what has this tiny island of long-lifers got to do with making better decisions? Well, according to Blue Zones researcher Dan Buettner, one of a handful of reasons that Okinawans live so long is the value they place on understanding and knowing their 'Ikigai' or 'reason for being'. As a western society, we tend to see work as a necessary chore. An essential, but mundane, part of our existence that stands between us and what we really want to be doing with our time. Our society envisages a clear distinction between what is work and what is not. We talk of 'pre' and 'post' retirement, 'work' and 'play', with the two constantly at odds with one another.

Okinawans, however, take an entirely different approach. Work is an integral part of life, so much so that they don't even have a word for retirement. They believe that searching for and discovering your reason for being is key to living a fulfilled and meaningful life. This isn't about what other people think you ought to do or what society views as best. Ikigai creates a framework for you to work out what success looks like on your terms.

Critically, it's not just asking you to define success as one dimensional. It recognizes that there are different components to a 'successful' life, and each means different things to different people.

One way of interpreting the concept of Ikigai is in this diagram. It deconstructs the various components of a fulfilled working life: doing work you love, providing something the world needs, earning money and being good at whatever you choose to do.

IKIGAI

I'm not suggesting that you use this concept to identify a single passion or job that you must tirelessly pursue for the rest of your days. That kind of thinking is unhelpful, not to mention idealistic; what might be right now, might not be in ten years. The 'follow your passion' philosophy is enticing – who doesn't want to pursue something that doesn't feel like work? But save for child prodigies who reach Grade 8 violin at the age of twelve or the genius mathematician destined to become a Nobel Prize winner, the vast majority of humankind really has no idea as to what they should do with their life, let alone what their 'passion' is. Most of us are just bumbling along, hoping we stumble into something that we quite like doing. However, unhelpfully, much of the self-help chatter would have us believe that somewhere in the cosmos is this single thing called our 'passion' just waiting to be found. Whilst this might be a wonderfully romantic idea for those that have 'found' their *raison d'être*, it's an ideology that for many is totally crippling.

Finding meaningful work that aligns with your model of success isn't a destination at which you finally get to kick off your Louboutins, gaze out of your corner office and live happily ever after. Being content with your work isn't a black and white thing or a moment of enlightenment. Success is a process.

DO THIS >
1. WHO ARE YOU?

The first step to applying the principle of Ikigai is to work out who *you* actually are. How do each of the components relate to your model of success and what does a success-ful working life look like? You can't do anything about un-happiness unless you know what happiness looks like.

Take four pieces of paper and for each of the following components write what comes to mind. Use the example questions as prompts if needed.

1. **What I love** – e.g. think back to a time at work or school when time flew and work felt effortless. What kind of work really energizes you? What kind of work do you really hate? What could you not do on a daily basis?
2. **What I can be paid for** – e.g. how much money is enough? (We'll come back to this on pp. 55–6) Do you like expensive things?

3. **What the world needs** – e.g. who inspires you – what is it about them you admire? What are your values? What do you feel strongly about? What is injustice?

4. **What I'm good at** – e.g. what have you found easier than other people? What do people ask you for advice with? What did you do well at in school?

Reflect on the four areas and write down anything that comes to mind. If you get stuck, try to think as far back as when you were a kid: what did you really enjoy doing? What subjects came more naturally than others? Ignore any niggly thoughts such as 'ah but that was just luck' or 'that skill won't earn me any money', just write it down, however obscure it might be.

Once you've completely exhausted all of your answers, try to identify any overlapping themes.

Remember, this isn't meant to be a tick-box exercise in which a job either offers these things or it doesn't. Instead, think of each of the four components as being on a spectrum. For example, right now you might have a job you don't really love, that pays you more than enough, is sort of meaningful and that you're really great at. The thinking is that by understanding what's important to you and what you have and don't have in your current situation, you can get closer to your idea of success.

2. ASSESS YOUR CURRENT WORK LIFE

Think about your current job and where you sit on the four spectrums. If you're still at school or university and haven't started work yet, you can skip this one

It's important to say that you might not need your job to provide everything. Maybe you get satisfaction from other areas of your life. For example, volunteering might give you the sense of providing something the world needs.

I love my job

_____

Disagree   Agree

I am paid my ideal income

_____

Disagree   Agree

In my view my job provides something the world needs

_____

Disagree   Agree

I'm really good at my job

_____

Disagree   Agree

So, rather than seeing success and happiness as something attainable only once you've found your 'passion', instead, we need to see being successful as something we do on our terms and as a lifelong work in progress. Rather than trying to find your 'dream job', it's about understanding what your definition of success looks like and then moving towards it.

Step 3: Think five years

...you keep taking jobs that you don't like because you think it will look good on your resume. Isn't that a little like saving up sex for your old age?

Warren Buffett

For those who know what they want to do, particularly with vocational careers like medicine, having a long-term career plan makes sense; there are precise hoops to jump through, qualifications to earn and times when decisions need to be made. However, for most careers, the need for a long-term plan just doesn't apply. As our working lives become more fluid, we have the potential to forge our own career paths in our own way. In fact, creating a traditional career plan just doesn't make sense; we know just how rapidly the world is changing and so are we. There's a very real possibility that what we might imagine ourselves doing in ten years could either no longer exist, or not be what we want anymore.

But I LOVE to plan. Any opportunity to strategize, hypothesize and optimize and I'm there. The idea of letting go and embracing uncertainty is, frankly, terrifying. As humans, we're fundamentally uncomfortable with the unknown and are hard-wired to remove the discomfort of not knowing what the future holds.

The risk with thinking too far into the future is that we start to see time as operating within the same bounds as money; whilst you can invest money in the hope of getting more back, the same can't be said for the years we spend working. Of course, investing time can create opportunities which mean you can spend your time differently. For example, investing seven years of life into medical school provides the returns of being able to practise as a doctor. But, unlike money, you really can't make any more than you already have.

After years of formal education and qualifications that promise to take you further, when we get to the workplace it's tempting to adopt a similar mindset: take jobs that you don't want to be in but that are 'good for your CV' and promise to bump you up the next rung of the ladder. To some extent this is good practice. We all have to start somewhere and particularly early on it's inevitable that there will be a fair chunk of mundanity that we have to tolerate and aspects of our jobs that we just don't like.

But where do we draw the line? At what point does living for the weekend become living for retirement? When do we take a job because that's what we actually want to be doing rather than one that we manage to pull ourselves through? The risk is, we never do. We spend our entire working life putting our own happiness on hold in the hope that, one day, we'll cash in and reap the benefits of our exceptional ability to put off doing what we actually want. Warren Buffett likens taking jobs to build your CV to saving up sex for old age: 'There comes a time when you ought to start doing what you want. Take a job that you love.' This isn't to say we should always take the easy road and only do the things that will make us happy right now. If that were the case I'd be eating a New York cheesecake for breakfast. In your twenties learning should be a priority and, a lot of the time, learning is boring and painful. However, to avoid the 'living for retirement' trap we need an end goal in sight; a destination to head towards, and one that is possible to reach in the next three to five years.

Step 4: So you want to be rich

Whoever says that money can't buy happiness can transfer theirs to my bank account right now. Whilst the saying is often wheeled out in an attempt to make us feel better about our own measly salaries, let's be honest, money is useful. There are a plethora of studies on the subject but the general consensus is that yes, money does contribute to our overall wellbeing, but only up to a point. Studies have produced different results but it seems that beyond an individual income of around £35,000, more money starts to have increasingly little impact on our happiness whilst a sense of purpose, family and health all become more important. Of course, this is a huge generalization with a multitude of individual differences that might affect how much money you need to reach peak happiness. Living in a wealthy country, an expensive city or having a family will mean you're more likely to require a higher salary before reaching contentment. However, the general principle that the positive effect of money happiness starts to trail off beyond a certain point, appears to apply to everyone.

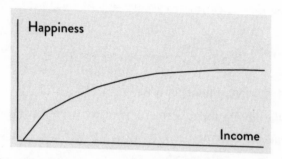

Whilst the money and happiness debate is a complicated one, the societal attitudes towards having it tend to be much more binary. When it comes to how we talk about it, there are two positions that dominate our culture. At one end, the anti-wealth sentiment that views money as the lowest form of good, and at the other the total glorification and endless pursuit of 'more'. Where's the middle ground that makes it OK to say you'd like more cash without feeling like a total money grabber? More money is only dangerous when it no longer becomes a tool by which to meet the needs in your life, but a need in itself. Something that is required to maintain a part of ourselves, be it our social status, power or success.

Rather than let culture tell you how you should feel about money, decide for yourself. In the Ikigai diagram on p. 47, doing something you can be paid for is one of the traits of a successful working life, but the question is, how much does money motivate you? And how much do *you* want and need to be paid? Understanding this is not only helpful in making career choices but it's also a powerful way to rein in any limitless ambitions of just wanting to be 'f******* loaded'!

So what is the difference between your wants and needs? And how do you calculate your own?

DO THIS > YOUR IDEAL INCOME

1. Define your financial needs

Needs – Expenditure that I require to live a physically and mentally healthy life

Look over your spending from the last one to three months and add up any spending that you'd describe as a 'need'. This is your **necessary income** – the amount you need each month to have a physically and mentally healthy life. If you're in the tricky position of struggling to afford your needs, think about what's currently missing and add this to your current total.

2. Define your financial wants

Wants – Expenditure that would make life more enjoyable, comfortable and enable you to prepare for the future

Next, add up any spending you'd describe as a 'want'.

Imagine a world where nobody sees what you have or how you spend your money. This isn't about what you think you should have or what would look good to other people – there'll always be more of that.

Instead focus on the things that would give you continual satisfaction.

What else would make *your* life easier, more enjoyable,

more comfortable and help you prepare for the future? For some this might be a holiday, for others it could be affording a blow dry every month.

3. Add your 'goals'

Goals – The money you put aside for your long-term goals

If you're using the 50:30:20 budgeting method (we'll get onto this in 'Spend it', pp. 152–60), this should make up around 20 per cent of your post-tax income.

How to calculate your goals:

$$=(0.2 \times (\text{financial wants} + \text{financial needs})) / 0.8$$

4. Calculate your ideal income

Needs + *Wants* + *Goals* = IDEAL INCOME (POST-TAX)

This is your ideal income; a rough guide to the amount of money (post-tax) you'd like to have in order to live your best financial life. When it comes to earning, making sure you've got your financial needs met goes without saying but keeping an eye on your ideal income also gives you permission to want and aspire for more. Who doesn't want cool things!? Knowing what you would *ideally* want to earn also helps you to make better decisions about your career and be realistic about the kind of work you do. If you've got a sky-high 'ideal income' then it might be more challenging to enjoy a lower-paying job, so think about what has to give. Are you being realistic about your wants or do you need to look at a different industry that pays better? How much do *you* care about money?

Step 5: Take action

The enemy of success isn't failure, it's inaction.

The purpose of Step 2 was to both define your ideal working life and to look at where you are now. But it's only with action that you'll get from one to the other.

When I imagined my career on the mountain of doom, taking action seemed impossible. What if I made the wrong choice? How about all the other things I could do? I could never do that! But work just isn't like that. It's only by doing, trying, moving, questioning and more doing that we can test our thinking and learn more about ourselves.

Not only is it in the action that you get closer to your best working life, but it's actually *in* the movement towards a goal that you feel good, not at the end. Think about how incredible it feels when you've had a really productive day and ticked things off your list. It's not necessarily because we've accomplished anything huge, or reached a major milestone, but because we're closer to something we want. Getting there is just the icing on the cake but if you don't enjoy the process you're aiming at the wrong thing.

PART 2: MAKING CHANGES

Good decisions come from experience, and experience comes from bad decisions.

Mark Twain

At some point or another we're going to question whether the decisions we've made are the right ones. What might have been right then, isn't always right now and, sometimes, it takes trying something to realize that it's not your jam. You'll change, industries change and companies change.

In the next section, we'll look at making career changes: from 'tweaks' to total 'OMFG, what on earth am I doing with my life?!' redirections.

Get the basics right

Knowing that things aren't quite right in your current job may well mean that you're in the wrong career altogether but there might be something more fundamental missing. When we think about what a 'good job' is, what springs to mind? An industry? Skillset? Qualification? Job title? Pay grades? These are of course important and defining factors, but it's easy to overlook the basic stuff: the fundamental things we need to be happy at work.

Before you go all quarter-life crisis, it's worth assessing whether there are any fixes that can be made within your existing job or career. Researchers looking at what makes us satisfied at work have identified five key needs that must be met in order for us to be content with our jobs. These aren't career or personality specific, they're of universal importance, regardless of who you are or what your ambitions might be. So, whilst you may have found your perfect job, without these, the chances are you'll struggle to stay happy long term.

Supportive colleagues	☑
Job insecurity	☑
Pay you feel is unfair	☑
Very long hours	☑
A reasonable commute	☑

1. A reasonable commute

No one likes a long commute, in fact it's this very hatred that is one of the main drivers behind property prices. In London, every minute further away from the centre produces an average saving of £3,048. Yet for most, a commute is an unavoidable part of working life, with the average UK worker spending four hundred days commuting. Not only does a longer commute lead to poor work satisfaction but it's also responsible for poor mental and physical health, with the worst hit being those who travel over an hour by bus.

What can you do about it?

I'm under no illusion that, with exorbitant rents, a longer commute is unavoidable for pretty much any city-dweller, but to what extent are you saving money at the cost of your precious time and perhaps happiness? Suppose you are saving an extra £50 a month by living a further twenty minutes away from work. If that's money you have, and you've taken care of all the basics, then calculate the opportunity cost of saving that £50. For example, an extra forty minutes a day spent commuting is over thirteen hours a month. With time being our most precious resource, would you value your thirteen hours at £50? Think about what else you could do with your time. Perhaps you could even work a little longer in preparation for that promotion or start your business on the side.

2. Very long hours

Employers will harp on about work–life balance but often the practice falls a little short of the preaching. Although most employment contracts will promise a comfortable forty-hour week, workplace culture and expectations around working hours vary hugely from job to job. It's normal to experience a 'busy season' or periods of growth when recruitment hasn't yet caught up with the increased workload. However, if you find yourself endlessly bailing on post-work drinks with friends, struggling to fit in any exercise or time for yourself, it might be worth evaluating if your work–life balance is in need of some attention.

What can you do about it?

Naturally, some industries have different demands and expectations when it comes to working hours. To some extent, this is correlated with salary. Working in finance, for example, you can probably expect to be working well before and beyond the 9–5 working day. So, providing you enjoy your job, what are the hours you'd be willing to work? There is absolutely no shame in deciding that, actually, long hours just aren't for you. Also, look at the lives of colleagues five years ahead of you. Do they have the kind of work–life balance that you'd be happy with?

If your hours aren't the norm for your industry then you might be stuck in a company that's either under-resourced or is battling an unhealthy culture of presenteeism. Originally used to describe employees coming into work whilst being unwell, presenteeism describes a negative culture of employee disengagement. The Chartered Institute of Personnel Development (CIPD) describes how its roots are usually found in fears over job security, worry of being perceived as lazy or senior management putting operational efficiency before staff morale. Sound familiar? If so, your first port of call should be to raise the issue with your line manager or HR and, if possible, get consensus from your colleagues to see if they feel the same way. However, workplace cultures run deep so, if all else fails, it might be time to look for pastures new. Start eyeing up other companies within your industry and be sure to get objective opinions on the ins and outs of their expectations around working hours.

3. Pay you feel is unfair

It hurts. In practical terms, our salary feels like a reflection of our worth, so to discover that someone doing the same job is being paid more feels like a slap to the face. In the UK, the past couple of years have seen an important rise in conversation and action around how companies pay their employees. This has culminated in legislation which means companies with more than 250 employees are legally obliged to publish their gender pay gap figures. However, there's a big difference between equal pay and a gender pay gap:

> **Equal pay** – Means that men and women in the same company performing equal work must receive equal pay, as set out in the Equality Act 2010. Employees are entitled to have a salary that is as favourable as those of a 'comparator' in the company. Comparator means a current employee that carries out work that is 'of equal value', 'broadly similar' or 'rated as equivalent'.

> **Gender pay gap** – Is a measure of the difference between men and women's average earnings across an organization or the labour market. It is expressed as a percentage of men's earnings. In Britain, there is an overall gender pay gap of 18.1 per cent.

What can you do about it?

Dealing with pay you feel is unfair is complex. In the abstract, we should be able to voice concerns without jeopardizing our career prospects, but the sad truth is, oftentimes, it just doesn't work like that. If you believe that you're being paid below the industry average this is less complex. Gather evidence from recruiters and salary websites to build a strong case that you can take up at your next performance review. Moving across to another company is also a great way to secure a pay rise. If, on the other hand, you think you might be subject to unequal pay, you are well within your right to take action, but it's worth treading carefully. If you've got your suspicions that you're not alone, then it can be helpful to build collective support and evidence. Unequal pay claims can get messy so make sure you follow your company's procedures and use the appropriate HR channels. That being said, remember that, ultimately, the purpose of HR is to protect the company so, if you exhaust all routes and make no headway, you may want to get independent legal support.

4. Job insecurity

Being just a little bit worried about your job security is normal – but when you've that gut feeling something's up, there are rumours of redundancy or you're no longer invited to important meetings, then it's understandable that alarm bells might be ringing.

What can you do about it?

Focusing on what you can control is the best strategy when it comes to tackling fears of job insecurity. Rather than letting fear paralyse you, turn it into positive energy and create a game plan for yourself. At work, remain confident, professional and keep doing a great job. Check your employment contract for details on notice periods and be clear on your rights. Off duty, build a back-up plan, identifying new jobs you could apply for and think strategically about how you can turn this into something great. Sometimes redundancy can be a blessing in disguise. Maybe this is the kick you needed to do that thing you've always wanted.

5. Supportive colleagues

In an early episode of the UK series *The Office* the unsuspecting Gareth returns to his desk to find his stapler suspended in lemon jelly, a prank that, understandably, his colleagues find hilarious. Jelly pranks aside, getting along and having a laugh with your colleagues is one of the best bits of work. When it's likely you'll spend more time with your colleagues than you will with your significant other, parents, best friend, siblings and cat, you want to be damn sure that you actually like them. Negative workplace relations can be a catalyst for misery for everyone involved. Not only does liking your colleagues make work fun, but their support can be super helpful for your career development.

What can you do about it?

Employers touting their unique workplace culture isn't just in vain. It genuinely matters. You might be utterly brilliant at your job but if you don't connect with your colleagues, work life can be so much harder than it need be. What kind of culture do you thrive in? Do you like boozy post-work drinks on a Thursday? Or are you more about reading your book at lunchtime? What kind of environment will make you productive and motivated to come into work every day? When you're job hunting, don't be enticed by the promise of nap stations and prosecco on tap, do some digging to figure out what, exactly, the company culture is. If need be, go into stealth mode and track down previous employees to see why they left and scour the internet for honest reviews.

If you don't feel supported in your current job, make sure you've exhausted all avenues before throwing in the towel. Is there a senior colleague you could ask for career advice or who could act as a mentor figure? They'll be flattered you asked and are bound to have valuable insights and connections that you can learn from.

Big changes

If you don't like something, change it. If you can't change it, change your attitude.

Maya Angelou

Change is good. The only problem: it's scary as hell. We're hard-wired to resist it and find any excuse to stay exactly where we are. Evolutionarily speaking, this makes complete sense. If our current situation brings us no danger, provides a roof over our heads and keeps us fed, our inner caveman is chill. The last thing he wants is for you to go shaking things up, quitting your job and placing your hard-earned security and safety on the line. He'd much prefer the predictable but secure shittiness of your current situation over the unpredictable but possible greatness that might come with changing things. He couldn't give a damn as to whether you've defined your Ikigai or discovered your purpose. As a result, we can find ourselves torn between the security of our current life and what we really want to be doing, spending far too long in jobs and situations that really don't make us happy. Not only does Neanderthal-you do a great job in convincing you that really you'd be much better off sticking with the jobs you hate, he's also a massive pessimist and will greatly exaggerate the risk associated with making a big change. He'll wildly exaggerate the odds of something going wrong and 'catastrophize' the possible consequences, conjuring up horrific worst-case scenarios.

Behavioural scientists call the effect of this the status quo bias: our innate preference for keeping things as they are by doing nothing as opposed to changing the course of action and making a new decision. Behavioural economists Kahneman and Tversky put this down to our tendency to want to minimize regret at all costs; we'd feel much more regret if we made a decision and it went badly, than if we didn't make one at all but the consequences were just as terrible. Whilst this behaviour might have kept us out of harm's way in a Stone Age era of lions and tigers, it is nothing but unhelpful today. When it comes to our careers, it's this kind of thinking that not only tempts us towards inaction, but leads us to resign ourselves to the fact that we couldn't dream of going after what we really want.

We've all seen this mechanism in action – think of that friend who will tirelessly divert every conversation back to their awful job, yet never does anything about it. Or the one who has a million business ideas that they never pursue. It's not easy to escape this kind of mindset. Embracing change and taking action is a painful process but, with practical and realistic thinking, it is possible.

What if I fall? Oh, but my darling, what if you fly?

Erin Hanson

Let it go

One reason that we're so resistant to making big changes is that it involves accepting that we may have unnecessarily invested our time and energy in something that we no longer want. Changing course feels like starting from scratch; precious time, literally poured down the drain. I know how tempting it is to stay put and hope that, with a promotion or a pay rise, we might feel different and things might change, but it's this kind of thinking that is the biggest threat to our time and happiness.

One very real example of the dangers of clinging onto our original plan is the story of the infamous Polaroid camera company. Back in the sixties and early seventies, business was booming for Polaroid, with sales accounting for around 20 per cent of the US market for film and photography. They were the Apple of their day and, at their peak, had over 21,000

employees. Founder Edwin Land was a revolutionary and a sci-
entist. He dedicated the majority of his life to researching and
developing the best instant photography processes, determined
to make it possible for a picture to be taken and developed in
sixty seconds or less. He succeeded, however; as the eighties ap-
proached, digital camera technology began to take off. Whilst
Polaroid did make some investments in digital, Land had in-
stilled an anti-electronic culture in the company. So much time,
effort and energy had been invested in developing the best instant photographic technology around that he refused to accept
that things needed to change. His strategy and business model
rested on the principle that customers would always want physical photographs to remember events, not just digital ones. The
idea that this might no longer be true ran counter to everything
Land stood for and the principles he had built his company on.
The need to change tack was too difficult to accept, eventually
resulting in the company filing for bankruptcy in 2001.

The tendency to stick with past ideas and decisions, even
when new evidence or events makes doing so irrational, is
known as the commitment bias, and it's not just businesses
that make this mistake. To maintain pride, we do anything to
avoid appearing inconsistent. We like sticking to our guns and
believing that we've made great decisions, even if, in reality, we
know it would be better for us to make a different one. We often
approach the need for a career change in the same way. Despite
knowing deep down that we need to do something different,
we can't help but think about all the time and money that we've
invested just to get where we are now. In *Too Much Invested to
Quit*, psychologist Allan Teger comments on the Vietnam War:

'The longer the war continued, the more difficult it was to justify the additional investments in terms of the value of possible victory. On the other hand, the longer the war continued, the more difficult it became to write off the tremendous losses without having anything to show for them.' We struggle with the same battle, cringing at the thousands spent on a university degree or the years invested in a particular industry. It's painful to accept that our resources could have been better invested elsewhere. In business, economists refer to these losses as 'sunk costs': irrecoverable expenses that we simply cannot get back. However, continue to think of your career like a business you're investing in, and it's not all so bleak. Whilst there may have been some losses, you will have almost certainly made some gains from your investment of time. Be it making great contacts, picking up a brand name for your CV, learning a new skill, earning some money, gaining a decent degree that can be applied elsewhere or, at the very least, learning about yourself and what you don't want to do. Just like a business, the key to long-term career success and happiness is to know when to stop investing in your old decisions and make new ones. Don't be a Polaroid and resist change out of fear of what you might lose; write off the sunk costs, be thankful for the gains and start to invest your resources elsewhere.

You're not behind

It was 1955 Louisville, Kentucky, and sixty-five-year-old Harland had decided to retire. He'd had a string of jobs, from steam engine stoker to insurance salesman to petrol station operator and a number of business failures to boot. In a state of hopelessness and regret, he put pen to paper, began to write his will and contemplated suicide. He thought about what life might have been, about his love of cooking and how he'd wished he'd made more of this skill. He knew he had talent; whilst running a motel he'd developed a secret chicken recipe which had been a massive hit with his customers. There was clearly demand for his delicious fried chicken. Dragging himself out of his despair and gloom, and with only $105 to his name, Harland decided to start a franchise business. He began selling his chicken recipes to restaurants around the country and in just a few years the company expanded to more than 600 locations. By 1964, then seventy-three years old, he sold the Kentucky Fried Chicken corporation for $2 million (around $16 million in today's money).

The tale of KFC is a great example of how it really is never too late to start again. Behind so many stories of success are long, messy roads of redirection, failure and doubt. Wanting to make a change not only requires us to overcome a whole load of practical barriers, but psychological ones too. We worry about what other people will think, how it might dent our pride or put us behind our friends. We're particularly prone to this kind of thinking in our twenties; a time which can feel akin to a sort of arms race. Mission: graduate, get employed, coupled up and earning decent money ASAP. It's no wonder then, upon realizing that we're not where we want to be, that the idea of making a big change feels like a huge step backwards. A walk of shame back to the start line of 'The Great Career Sprint'. The truth is, there is a competition, but it's not how you imagine it. The moment you start to see life as a track race and let your eyes stray into the lane of someone else is the moment you start to lose. The real race is against yourself: do you have the courage to run at what you really want? It's sixty-year-old you that you should be worried about, not what your peers, parents or great aunt Jude might think. Whether it's a business venture, a new job or a total career change, make it the choice that defines who you become, not the opportunity you missed.

Embrace your story

After nourishment, shelter and companionship, stories are the thing we need most in the world.

Philip Pullman

Humans live for stories. It's why we can't get enough of *Love Island,* why politicians get elected and why criminals escape jail. Stories represent the randomness and suspense that comes with life. If life were predictable, there'd be no tales to tell. Stories help us to develop our own sense of identity and allow us to connect with one another. We can also leverage the power of storytelling in our own careers. Take the story of Colonel Harland Sanders. His story of chaos and depression prior to starting KFC wasn't something he managed to escape from, it was *part of* his success. The KFC brand hasn't shied away from Harland's messy backstory, sending in scurrying teams of PR agents to gloss over his mess. They've wholeheartedly embraced it. So much so that even after the company was purchased, Harland became a salaried brand ambassador, telling his story across the globe. Harland passed away in 1980, yet to this day people like me continue to share it.

Career changes can feel chaotic, like we've derailed with no clear destination ahead. However, gone are the days of smooth upward career trajectories. Change is the only certainty and never more so than for our generation's careers.

When Emma Rosen realized that her hard-earned and prestigious graduate job wasn't what she wanted to do after all, she decided to go on a quest to work out what she really wanted to 'be'. In what some might consider career suicide, she handed in her notice and went on what she describes as a 'Radical Sabbatical': spending a year trying twenty-five careers before turning twenty-five. Emma put her childhood dreams into action, sampling a variety of jobs including archaeology in Transylvania, tour guiding amid violent protests in Venezuela, investigative journalism with a national newspaper and being an extra in a major movie. Emma's 'why not' attitude hasn't been to the detriment of her career at all, in fact it's defined it. Her adventure is testament to the power of just giving things a go that she now works as a writer and speaker, telling her story to companies and schools throughout the UK.

Embrace your story with open arms and learn how to turn your own chaos into a damn good tale. Rather than seeing your career change as starting from scratch, try to weave in your backstory and use it to your advantage. What was it that inspired the change? Have you been through any particularly challenging times to get to where you are now? How would your previous experience be relevant to what you want to do next? Creating your own narrative not only helps you to become more memorable but will also build connections with other people. Your story is your most powerful asset and will set you apart from everyone else.

The F word

I am an old man and have known a great many troubles, but most of them never happened.

Mark Twain

The adage 'fail to plan, plan to fail' still holds true, and never more so than for making career changes. Often, the biggest psychological barrier we encounter is fear. Fear of failure, fear of regret, fear of judgement. They're all powerful emotions that can quickly reduce us to quivering wrecks unless handled properly. Change is stressful but start to unpick your fears and you'll find that what really lies at the heart is a fear of uncertainty; you have no idea what the future holds. You can throw yourself at something new with all the enthusiasm in the world, and still not be sure how it's all going to turn out. We have to accept that there are variables and influences out of our control. However, by identifying our fears, and separating the things we have control over from those we don't, they start to become just a little bit less scary. We begin to see that what, in our mind, might be an 'OMG' catastrophic eventuality may actually be a fairly resolvable 'meh'. Entrepreneur and author Tim Ferriss describes this as 'Fear Setting'.

DO THIS > DEFINE YOUR FEARS

1. First, start thinking about the real risks of making a change, how you can prevent them from happening and what you could do if the worst were to happen. Answer the questions below:

- **Action** – What is the change you want to make? (e.g. retrain to become a psychotherapist)
- **Define** – What could go wrong and what are you most scared of?
- **Prevent** – How could you prevent that fear from coming true?
- **Repair** – What could you do if it did happen?

2. What might be the benefit of a partial success or attempt? (e.g. you would learn a new skill and become more employable)

3. What is the cost of inaction?

- In six months
- In one year
- In three years

Easy choices, hard life. Hard choices, easy life.

Jerzy Gregorek

PART III

START IT

A brief history of 'starting it'

Helping people to 'be their own boss' is big business in itself. Littered across the internet you'll find guides and gurus promising to teach you the secrets of financial freedom, four-hour work weeks and self-employment. This heightened interest is telling: as many find themselves resisting traditional models of employment, we are increasingly drawn to alternative means of making money. More than ever, we want to 'start' something: 70 per cent of twenty-five- to thirty-four-year-olds have ambitions to start a business, with financial success, freedom and independence being the biggest drivers.

Of course, being entrepreneurial isn't a new phenomenon that is unique to our time. We can trace our entrepreneurial footprints all the way back to 17,000 BC in New Guinea, where we find the earliest signs of business venturing. Local tribesmen spotted a demand for obsidian, a precious material used to make tools, which they would exchange for other useful materials such as animal skins and food. By 10,000 BC the Agricultural Revolution had begun, marking a real turning point in the history of entrepreneurship. As villages and towns began to sprawl across fertile ground, land owners saw an opportunity:

rather than foraging and hunting for their own dinner, why not specialize in one specific crop and provide enough supply for the entire community. Meanwhile, the rest of the population could specialize in other products, such as tools or shelter, which they would then trade for food. Over thousands of years, marketplaces and other infrastructures developed around these specialist activities, creating a hotbed for innovation, competition and new business.

Whilst the entrepreneurs of the Middle Ages might not have donned the same tortoiseshell glasses and combed beards that we associate with the startup scene of today, within every culture throughout time, there have always been those who have spotted opportunities to do things differently and challenge the status quo. That being said, perhaps today, where traditional employment appears not to tick our boxes in the way it might have a few decades ago, we have a far greater incentive to get in touch with our own entrepreneurial spirit. Many of us are intrigued by alternative working lives and, in a lot of cases, as pressure on our disposable incomes only increases, thinking entrepreneurially has become a necessity in order to make ends meet. Technology plays a part too. Website building platforms, online marketplaces and crowdfunding sites are just a handful of innovations that have dramatically lowered the barriers to both starting and running a business.

We're wanting to do our own thing, and sooner: the average age of a first-time founder is now twenty-seven as opposed to the thirty-five-year-old average of the baby boomer generation. However, the jury is still out as to whether we are putting our money where our mouths are. Although we have more entrepreneurial ambition, in reality we are starting fewer businesses than any previous generation. There is a reality gap; we admire entrepreneurs deeply, having grown up with TV staples such as *The Apprentice* and *Dragon's Den*, yet in practice we don't follow through.

And of course, not everyone wants to be an entrepreneur and that's cool. If we all quit the 9–5 with the hope of becoming the Zuckerbergs and Bezoses of tomorrow, the economy would grind to a halt. As we looked at in 'Earn it', understanding *your* model of success is what matters. Whether that means climbing a career ladder, going freelance or starting a tech company, it's about the kind of working life you want to live. If you can't think of anything worse than living the startup life or going freelance, no problem. Move right on to Part IV.

So, what about those who do want to do their own thing but haven't yet? Why isn't their entrepreneurial ambition translating into action? Well, ironically, one of the major barriers is the very same one that drives us into wanting to start businesses in the first place: the good old income–living-cost squeeze. There simply isn't the financial breathing space to start a business. We want and need to earn more and see doing our own thing as one route to achieving that, but at the same time don't feel financially secure enough to make the leap. It's a vicious cycle. Gone are the days of funding your business by re-mortgaging your house – chances are there is no house to re-mortgage and, for most city dwellers, paying rent is hard enough never mind stashing away a few grand in a 'maybe one day I'll start a business' fund.

But there's also a psychological factor at play. In fact, it's arguably the single most influential yet underrated quality that determines not only your decision to start a business but a whole array of other decisions too. From the life changing: how you'll raise your child. To the mundane: what you'll have for lunch tomorrow. Our tolerance for risk sets the tone of our lives, with a high dose being the common factor that unites entrepreneurs. And it's not surprising, starting a business means swallowing an enormous upfront cost: loss of social status, financial security, time and much more, all in the hope that one day it *might* pay off. For some, this reads: 'Hell on earth', and others: 'Freedom!' – we're all on a spectrum. The reality is, not all of us have it in us to start a business but in a world where the entrepreneur has reached god-like status this can be an uncomfortable truth.

Like many things, our formative years play a huge role in shaping how we feel about taking risks, not only through the influence of our family but our social and economic environment too. The effects of national and global change, be it a financial crash, changes to student loans or taxation policy, trickle down into our personal finances and then into our minds.

For example, studies on risk and decision making have found under thirty-five-year-olds to be naturally more cautious when it comes to making risky choices such as starting a business. We've lived through at least one financial crisis and, the chances are, we've been impacted directly or indirectly by the damage; whether it's finding it difficult to get a job or seeing a family member struggle with redundancy. There's even evidence of some intergenerational differences, with those who graduated well after the crisis of 2008 significantly more likely to risk failure than those who graduated during or shortly after the financial crisis. Whilst we are most definitely resilient, having emerged from education into a competitive job market, the expectation of unpaid internships and low pay, we are tending to err on the side of caution when it comes to taking entrepreneurial risks. As much as we may talk of our longing to pack in the day job, often we end up sticking with the stable, traditional employment that we fought hard to get.

And this is a sensible approach. Doing anything outside the realms of traditional employment is a risky business. The statistics aren't encouraging: in the UK, four out of ten small businesses will fail, with 20 per cent doing so in their first year. The risk of failure is huge, so cutting through the glorification of the entrepreneur and carefully considering your risks, and whether you're willing to take them, is a good thing.

But, equally, inaction can be just as costly long term. We've all seen it: the colleague who talks about how much they loathe what they are doing, but, at the same time, stays put. Or the one who has this business idea and is going to leave, but just as soon as they've secured their next promotion. In every workplace there are people with huge desires and the ability to do their own thing, but, for one reason or another, too fearful to act on them. The problem is, we want it to feel right. We think that with the passage of time, more experience or another promotion, taking a risk will be easier. And sometimes that is true. However, for most, age only makes it more difficult. The more we progress at work, the more we have to give up and the incentives to stay where we are only grows. Personal commitments, mortgages and kids complicate things more. We're another rung up the career ladder, but not closer to what we actually want to be doing. A little richer and a little more important, but now burdened with the real cost of inaction: regret.

'Starting it' isn't just about building billion-dollar tech companies or online businesses (although it might be…). It can mean anything from going freelance, starting a business on the side, to becoming a social entrepreneur, or launching a company with Fortune 500 ambitions. It's fundamentally about creating opportunities to make money as opposed to seeking ones that already exist and, most importantly, managing risk well so that you maximize your chances of success.

So, whether you have burning entrepreneurial desire or just an inkling that starting *something* at *some* point might be of interest, then this chapter is for you.

Having ideas

Every child is an artist. The problem is how to remain an artist once we grow up.

Pablo Picasso

The natural ability to imagine things that don't yet exist is both strange and fascinating. This isn't a learned skill, we're all born with the power of imagination. In fact, as children we're brimming with it, with our imaginations totally unconstrained. A pile of old boxes becomes a galaxy-invading spaceship, an overgrown suburban garden transforms into a jungle bursting with endangered species or the bed in the spare room imagined as an army bunker and you, ready to lead the battle. Children don't ask permission to use their imaginations or worry about judgement or failure, they just do it.

As we navigate our way through rigorous education systems and out into the wild world of the workplace, the value and usefulness of the imagination starts to wane. Being able to imagine the impossible into existence, be it an army bunker or spaceship, no longer serves as useful. Instead, our imaginations are blunted by learned reality, and value is placed on knowing things about what we *know* to exist. Through trial and error we settle into reality and start to understand how to thrive within its boundaries (how to impress people, win friends, get a good job), emerging into adulthood as fully functioning humans with habits and behaviours that get us through life without making an absolute tit of ourselves (or at least on a less regular basis).

The problem is that, as we grow up, our vision starts to narrow. The world that we once toyed with and moulded in our imaginations becomes fixed. We come to exist within its boundaries and begin to accept that maybe things are just how they are. Operating in reality is a necessary part of survival and sticking to the beaten path works: why try something new when you can be right? Unfortunately, what's 'right' is also what's been done many times before, which means we could be missing out on the untrodden paths that lead to surprises and new ideas.

The gift of the entrepreneur can be boiled down to the ability to see the world not as static, but as a place that is malleable. One where you can use your imagination to see how you might change it and believe that you can. A place where what has been done before doesn't have to be done again; in fact, the chances are, there are new and better ways to do things, and you can be the one to lead the way.

In the words of Steve Jobs:

When you grow up you tend to get told that the world is the way it is and your life is just to live your life inside the world. Try not to bash into the walls too much. Try to have a nice family life, have fun, save a little money... Life can be much broader once you discover one simple fact: Everything around you that you call life was made up by people that were no smarter than you. And you can change it, you can influence it... Once you learn that, you'll never be the same again.

Problems: Where good ideas exist

Having good business ideas isn't so much about thinking of them but more about letting your imagination create solutions where problems currently exist. Or, in the words of Richard Branson: 'identifying a gap in the market and creating a product of use to fill that hole and make people's lives better'. In fact, trying to think of business ideas is often where people go wrong. If we start by trying to find an idea, there's a tendency to think up a really great product and imagining a problem for it to solve. All great businesses identify the problem or need first and obsess over their potential customers, digging deep to truly understand what it is they want. Only then do they put pen to paper and try to build a solution. Paul Graham, founder of world-leading startup accelerator Y Combinator, believes that the number one reason startups fail is designing a product that nobody wants. It sounds so simple. Yet, time and time again, entrepreneurs expend all of their energy building something that in principle is incredible, without first checking to see if anyone actually needs it.

If problems and needs are where we find good ideas, how do we become better at spotting them and have the imagination to see how they might be solved? The good news is, having ideas is much more of a learned skill than a rare talent. We can see this in action by looking at the human brain. It's made of a network of over 100 billion interconnected neurons. How we think is simply a consequence of how all these neurons are connected. The further good news is, the brain isn't a static organ. It's ever changing and malleable, with an extraordinary ability to rewire and form new connections all the time. It's in these connections that new ideas are born.

So how do we make new connections and have great ideas? The secret is simple: change. Neuroscientists have found that by simply increasing the variety of our experiences, and changing up our environments, our brains rewire. It's when we continually throw ourselves into new places, with new people, that new ideas emerge. It's encouraging to think that all the companies you know and love today were, at one point, simply the spark of an idea, in a brain just like yours or mine.

Looking at how some of the world's most successful businesses started, there are also some clear patterns that we can use to direct our thinking and improve the odds that we'll have great ideas too.

1. Scratch your own itch

A classic entrepreneurial aphorism, 'scratching your own itch' means starting a business that solves a problem you have. When friends Joe and Brian talked about how they were struggling to pay their rent, they spotted an opportunity to make some cash: a design conference was about to open in San Francisco and all the hotels were fully booked. Within a single day they had set up airbedandbreakfast.com and within six they had a thirty-year-old Indian man, a thirty-five-year-old woman from Boston and a forty-five-year-old father of four from Utah sleeping on their living room floor. They'd spotted a problem that they wanted solved: the ability to make some quick money by welcoming total strangers into their home. Little did they know that their simple website would become the billion-dollar company that Airbnb is today.

2. Network

Steven Johnson, author of *Where Good Ideas Come From* (the bible of idea generation), is a huge proponent of what he calls 'liquid networks'. His theory is that great ideas don't emerge from a vacuum. Instead we need to put ourselves in an environment with people from different backgrounds and with different skill sets. 'What oftentimes turns the hunch into something bigger than a hunch is when your hunch collides with someone else's hunch,' Johnson says. This could mean joining an organized community such as a networking group or simply initiating more 'ideas-based' conversations with people different from you.

3. It's not about the money

'Chase the vision, not the money. The money will end up following you' are the wise words of Zappos' CEO, Tony Hsieh. Rarely are good businesses born from looking for ways to make money. Finding a customer and serving their need should be your number one. Make that your mission, do it well and the money will inevitably follow.

4. What's your niche?

You see things nobody else sees. If you've been working in a particular industry for some time, you will inevitably have been exposed to longstanding inefficiencies that are crying out for someone to tackle. For example, the story of Anne Boden, founder of Starling Bank. After rising to the top of the financial services industry, sitting in a number of high-profile positions in some of the UK's leading banks, Anne had grown frustrated by the restrictions still imposed by outdated technology. She saw an opportunity for change, a way of doing banking differently. So she did just that, starting her own digital bank from the ground up. Sounds impossible, right? In the four years since it was founded, Starling has become a serious player in the banking sector, challenging even the most established financial brands to change how they serve their customers.

5. Look into the future

Don't just think about existing problems or opportunities, instead think how our human wants and needs are going to change. Futurism is the practice of anticipating how things might be in the future, with Elon Musk being the absolute master. Whilst some may have initially scoffed at his wild propositions for space travel and electric vehicles, his bold predictions ensure that his products are the first to market, leaving well-established brands chasing at his feet. How do you think things will be in two, five or twenty years' time?

How to validate your ideas

The interesting thing about good business ideas is that whilst they are born out of imagination they also need to be grounded in reality. They need to paint a compelling picture of how things could be whilst also being plausible and able to exist in this world. For example, whilst we might sit on our delayed train imagining how useful a pocket-sized teleportation device would be, clearly science has some way to go before that's a possibility. One of the key traits of successful entrepreneurs is the ability to stand back and look objectively at the strengths and weaknesses of their ideas, and critically evaluate whether it's a plausible one. A bit like bad relationships, we can get so emotionally involved with an idea, so addicted to the possibility of running with it, that it's very easy to convince ourselves of its greatness. We fall victim to the confirmation bias: seeking and listening only to information that tells us what we really want to hear. That, 'Yes, Tinder for dogs is a brilliant idea, I can't possibly imagine why nobody has built it already!' So how do you fight against confirmation bias and assess whether your idea actually has legs in the real world?

This process of discovery is called 'Idea Validation' and not only ensures that you build a product or service that people actually want but saves you from needlessly spending your time and money on a bad idea.

Ask any entrepreneur and they'll tell you that the idea was the easy bit: the real work happens in the years after, when you battle to turn your idea into reality. So how do you work out whether your idea is worth ploughing all that time into? The following steps are a great starting point and will help you to establish if it's worth pursuing or not.

1. Know the competition

A few years ago, I had a business idea. Airbnb was beginning to take off in London and I noticed how flat owners in my block struggled to deal with the practicalities of managing short-term rentals. They didn't have the time to be worrying about cleaning or key handovers. With the glint of dollar signs in my eyes, I thought: imagine if a service existed that could take care of this for you. I'd spotted a genuine problem and thought up the perfect solution!

It was only after some rudimentary competitor analysis (a Google search) that my business dreams came crashing down. I realized that not one but several companies already existed: the market was crowded and I was too late.

Knowing your competition is vital to working out whether or not you should pursue an idea. That being said, don't be spooked at the first sight of competition. Most markets, from groceries to cars to cosmetics, have more than one player. In fact, it's this competition that keeps businesses innovating, ultimately delivering better value to you, the customer. But how do you know when competition is too much competition?

DO THIS >
1. GET TO KNOW THE COMPETITION

There are three key factors to look at:

- The size of the market (i.e. how many potential customers are there?)
- The current competition and what they do
- What could you do differently to serve the market better?

A second tool that will help you see how your business could succeed over others is a SWOT analysis. This is a tool that helps you identify the strengths, weaknesses, opportunities and threats within your business area.

- Strengths (what gives your company an edge over competitors or what is your Unique Selling Point?)
- Weaknesses (in what areas would your company be at a disadvantage?)
- Opportunities (how can you begin to capture market share and drive sales?)
- Threats (what are the barriers to entry that currently exist and how easily could a big player impose barriers once they identify you as a potential threat?)

By thinking objectively about these four components, you should start to get a picture of the current competitors, and whether there is a way for you to differentiate yourself. Equally, if there is absolutely no competition, question why and whether there is a market for your product at all.

2. FIND YOUR UNFAIR ADVANTAGE

It's the thing you have that your competition doesn't, and it can come in different shapes and sizes.

Unfair advantage could include but is not limited to:

- Experience – Do you have industry expertise that gives you a head start?
- Networks – Do you have a killer network that would help you launch your business?
- 1st Mover – Do you have the advantage of having spotted an opportunity first?
- Trade Secrets/Patents – Do you have a patented idea or insider knowledge?
- Speed – Are you able to design and build your business faster than anyone else?

2. Define your idea

We don't have a strategic plan. It's called doing things.

Herb Kelleher, Founder, Southwest Airlines

We can strategize, hypothesize and theorize all we like but, in truth, no business ever goes to plan. Starting a business is a fluid process: you win, lose, pivot, adjust and, most importantly, learn as you go. That's not to say you shouldn't have a plan of action; having a clear vision and goal is important. However, spending your time perfecting a lengthy business plan with complex financial projections isn't the way to go.

Many entrepreneurs now advocate taking a faster and more nimble approach: identifying your key assumptions and then testing them. In other words, quickly mapping out how and why you think your business might work, and then putting those thoughts to the test in the real world. This approach is called the Lean Startup methodology, established by entrepreneur Eric Ries, and looks at a new way of creating new businesses and getting your idea into the real world faster. His approach is all about rapidly testing, tweaking and launching products, minimizing the risk of making something that nobody wants.

One way to kick off the process is with the Lean Business Model Canvas (LBMC): a tool developed by Ash Maurya and used by entrepreneurs across the globe. The great thing about the LBMC is that it breaks down your business idea into bitesize segments. By exploring each of the components that make up your business, you'll be better able to spot weaknesses and opportunities. It also provides a great way to communicate your business to potential customers and investors.

DO THIS > COMPLETING THE LBMC

Use the following framework to define your business.

PROBLEM	SOLUTION	UNIQUE VALUE PROPORTION	UNFAIR ADVANTAGE	CUSTOMER SEGMENTS
What problem are you solving or customer need are you meeting?	How are you solving that problem or meeting that need?	What makes your business different?	What makes your business hard to copy? e.g. You have specialist knowledge, experience or information	Who are your target customers?
	KEY METRICS			
	What are the measurements you will use to monitor the success of your business? e.g. Sales, referrals etc.		CHANNELS	
			How are you going to target those customers? e.g. Instagram, events etc.	
COST STRUCTURE		REVENUE STREAMS		
What are the costs of setting up and running your business?		How are you going to make money?		
PRODUCT		MARKET		

GFY + UNDERSTANDING YOUR BUSINESS MODEL

The bottom two boxes of the LBMC are often the most intimidating for new entrepreneurs, yet they are arguably the most important. Your cost structure and revenue streams are what make up your business model: your step by step plan to make your business **profitable**.

So first, let's define what we mean by revenue, costs and profitability.

Revenue is the income earned by a business over a period of time, e.g. one month. The amount of revenue earned depends on two things – the number of items sold and their selling price. In short: **revenue = price x quantity**

- **Revenue streams** are the sources from which revenue is generated. For example, Netflix's main revenue stream is through subscriptions whilst Facebook's is advertising. Total revenue is all of the main revenue streams added up.

Costs are the expenses involved in making a product or delivering a service. There are two primary costs that make up total costs:

- **Variable costs** – These change depending on the amount of product being made.
- **Fixed costs** – These stay the same even if more is produced.

For example, a bakery's main variable cost would be flour, their fixed cost would be the rent on the bakery.

Profitability is a company's ability to use its resources to generate revenues that are higher than their costs.

Profit is found by subtracting total costs from revenue.

- In short: **profit = total revenue - total costs**.
- The point when total revenue is greater than total costs is called the 'break-even point'.
- If a company's total costs are higher than their total revenue, they make a loss. Whilst making a loss is normal for new and growing businesses, profitability is critical to any company's long-term survivability.

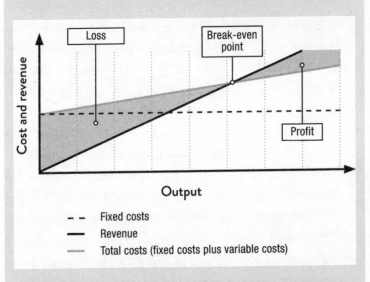

When filling out your LBMC, start by naming your revenue streams, fixed and variable costs. Using approximations, you can then start to put numbers to these. You'll then be able to answer questions such as:

- What is the amount required to run your company in a month?
- What will the price of your product or service be?
- How much of your product or service do you need to sell to break even?
- What are your revenue streams?

3. Test your idea

Once you've completed your LBMC, it's time to get testing. Given that you want your business to survive in the real world, your testing should be done there too! Serial entrepreneur Steve Blank calls this 'getting out the building'. You can create a beautiful brand and think about your idea all you like, but until you speak to potential customers you won't know if you are genuinely providing something they want. The process of customer discovery isn't about trying to sell to customers, it's about testing all the assumptions you've made in your LBMC and listening to them to see if you're right about their problems.

For example, let's say you're trying to start a new dog-walking service for people in your neighbourhood. On your canvas you may have noted the problem: 'Dog owners in my area struggle to find people to walk their dogs.' Now it's time to put it to the test: getting out there and speaking to your potential customers. One of the fatal mistakes that aspiring entrepreneurs make is to hear a few words of encouragement from friends and family, and call that 'research'. Your parents will always tell you it's a wonderful idea, so do the hard thing and seek objective honest feedback.

GFY + KNOW YOUR CUSTOMERS

*Get closer than ever to your customers. So close that you tell
them what they need well before they realize it themselves.*
Steve Jobs

One of the most important habits of successful entrepreneurs is really understanding their customers. To build a business that truly solves an existing problem, or meets a need, you have to understand who you are trying to serve. Your job is to understand them better than they understand themselves. Where do they hang out? What type of people are they? What brands do they love? What influences their purchasing decisions?

Once you've gathered all these details, you will then be able to determine the following:

- What is the market size – are there enough customers to create a sustainable business?
- How will you market your product or service to them?
- How will you price your product or service?

You can conduct research in a multitude of ways, from focus groups to surveys to one-on-one interviews. The internet now gives us access to some amazing research technologies, which can connect you to thousands of people who fit your target market, at the click of a button. However, many people find that a simple twenty-minute chat over a coffee is often the most insightful. This allows you to clarify your interviewees' answers but also gives you a chance to probe further and get to the real heart of the issue. Whichever form of research you choose, aim to interview at least thirty people who fit your target market. This should give you enough information to gauge if demand exists and, as a bonus, you might get some sign-ups!

The questions you ask will depend largely on your business but, as a starting point, use the following topics as a guide:

- Demographic information
- What their behaviours and habits are
- Where they encounter problems
- How they currently try to solve their issue/products they currently use
- What would their ideal solution/product be?
- What do they think about your idea and why wouldn't they like it?

Once you're done interviewing, review all your responses and draw out the key messages. Are there similar themes and problems people encounter? Does it confirm your assumptions made in the LBMC? If not, how could you change your business model to fit what your target market has told you? Once both your LBMC and your research align, you're ready to go to the next stage.

4. Testing, testing...

Just as you should be testing your idea in the real world, the same goes for your product. Although tempting, developing an entire product range before launch, or building more features for your app, doesn't optimize your time or money. Whilst your inner perfectionist might scream, the Lean Startup methodology calls for a 'quick and dirty' approach to building a product or service.

If you're building a tech product, this is often described as a Minimum Viable Product or MVP. An MVP is a product with just enough features to satisfy early customers, and to provide feedback for future product development.

Whilst MVP tends to be used to describe digital products, the same principle applies to physical products and real-life services. The question you should be asking yourself is: what is the smallest thing I can make or do that serves my customer in the simplest and cheapest way possible whilst also providing me with feedback?

For example, let's say you're starting a new low-sugar ice cream brand. The first thing you'd probably want to do is to make sure you have your core product at its absolute best. This means starting small: testing recipes in your kitchen, getting feedback and tweaking it until it's just right. You might then create a small batch and try to sell it at your local farmers' market or try to get it stocked at an independent retailer. Assuming this proves there was demand and you had some valuable feedback on how to improve, you might then hire an industrial kitchen and think about expanding your line.

The skill of a great poker player is knowing which hands to fold, in other words knowing how to lose the least. The same goes for great founders. The beauty of this approach is that it not only maximizes the chance of success but minimizes the losses too, saving you both time and money. If it turns out that your idea just doesn't have legs, you've not lost much. By continuously testing and tweaking your idea, it's also much easier to adapt it into something that does work.

5. Launching

When you've researched, tested, tweaked and tested some more, it's now time to get your product into your customers' hands. How you go about this all depends on your business; it might be overnight or a more gradual process. In the land of tech, being in 'beta' describes launching a product to a small group of customers first, getting feedback and then launching to a wider audience. Obviously this doesn't work for all businesses but the most important thing is to have a timeline and plan of what's happening and when. Of course, things never go to plan, but making sure you have key benchmarks and goals will help you stay on track.

Go fund your business

Just as we need money to stay alive, so do businesses. For some, raising money might not be an issue. Maybe you've been able to invest your own cash or have decided to bootstrap, where your business is able to fund itself. However, for many businesses, getting your hands on some external cash will be necessary to get your business off the ground and to grow it.

Here we'll look at the most popular sources of funding, broken down into three main categories: equity, debt and alternative funding.

1. Equity funding

Where money is invested and, in exchange, a slice of the

company is given to the investor. This slice is called 'equity'. The advantage is that there is no requirement to repay the investor if the business fails. The disadvantage is the owner has to give up a percentage of their business. This can mean losing some control over the company. Types of equity funding:

- **Friends and family** – Seeking funding from those you know, in exchange for equity in your business
- **Angel investors** – High-net-worth individuals with an interest in supporting and investing in businesses. Ideally with sector experience to be able to offer some guidance too
- **Equity crowdfunding** – Using an online platform to reach thousands of potential individual investors. Those who do invest each receive a very small portion of equity
- **Venture capitalists** – Firms which specialize in making large investments in early-stage businesses that are expected to deliver significant returns
- **Incubators and accelerators** – Programmes that provide both funding and practical support, designed to help you build and scale your business

2. Debt funding

Where money is lent and, in exchange, the lender will expect repayment at a later date. The advantages are that the owner retains full control and ownership of their company and interest repayments are paid pre-tax and therefore represent a tax saving. However, the disadvantage is that the business has an obligation to repay the lender. This can mean forcing the company into liquidation if they are unable to pay back the debt. Types of debt funding:

- **Friends and family** – Seeking funding from those you know, with the promise of paying it back at a later date
- **Bank loans/Small business lenders** – Financial institutions offering loans to small businesses. This is with the promise of paying it back at a later date, usually with high interest rates because of the increased risk
- **Asset financing** – Receiving a loan in exchange for promising assets owned by the business (e.g. property) in the instance that the business is unable to pay back the loan. Will generally have a lower interest rate than traditional bank loans because the bank has the security of the asset

3. Alternative funding

Outside of equity and debt funding, there are also some alternative sources that are worth exploring. Types of alternate funding:

- **Competitions** – Cash awarded to promising startups. Can also provide useful press coverage and exposure to investors
- **Bursaries and grants** – Cash provided by the government, universities or charitable organizations, often targeted at social enterprises or startups within a particular niche
- **Reward-based crowdfunding** – Investors pledge cash in

return for being sent a product at a later date, or in exchange for a reward such as a discount on future purchases

Five steps to launch

As if the psychological challenge of starting a business wasn't enough, you've then got the task of navigating your way through all the practical steps that come with it.

To get you started, this step by step list will help you get the foundations in place and prepared to start trading.

1. Choose your business structure

All businesses, from one-man/woman-bands, to FTSE 100 companies, must have a legal structure. It's this that determines many of the ways that your business operates, from how you're taxed to who is legally liable were anything to go wrong. In the UK, you've got four options to choose from:

- **Sole trader** – A self-employed person who is the sole owner of their business and is personally responsible for the business and its debts. The profit of the sole trader is calculated and then 'drawings' are taken from the business which are taxed as income. This is unlike a company where salaries are a cost of the business
- **Partnership** – A group of two or more individuals who share responsibility for the business and its debt. A partnership agreement outlines how the partnership will

be managed and how profits will be split. Partners are usually self-employed

- **Limited company** (LTD) – A business with its own legal identity, separate from its owners (shareholders) and managers (directors). After the company has paid corporation tax, shareholders can receive profits as dividends (can only be paid from retained earnings) and also pay themselves a salary. Owners are not personally responsible for the debts that the business cannot pay

- **Limited liability partnership** (LLP) – A group of two or more people who run the business but are not personally responsible for debts the business can't pay. How the profits and responsibilities are shared is decided in an LLP agreement. Partners are usually, but not necessarily, taxed as self-employed

GFY + A WORD ON... LIABILITY

Whilst the adage that 'those who fly solo have the strongest wings' may ring true for many entrepreneurs, understanding the risks of flying alone is vital. Glancing over each of the different structures, you'll see that each one gives its owners a different degree of responsibility for any debts that the company owes. The extent to which the owners or shareholders are responsible for any debts or losses made by the business is called your liability.

In the case of businesses that might need some external debt funding, this is a really important consideration.

In the case of limited companies and limited liability

partnerships, the owners have 'limited liability', meaning that if the business were to fail, only the company's assets would be used to pay back the debt. However, in the case of sole traders and partnerships, the owners of the business have 'unlimited liability' meaning that, if the business fails, their own personal assets (including their houses and savings) could be used to pay back the debt. This is a scary thought for many and is one of the main reasons that you may want to choose a structure with limited liability.

CHOOSING A STRUCTURE

TYPE	ADVANTAGES	DISADVANTAGES	BEST FOR...	NEXT STEPS
Sole trader	• Low cost, easy to set up • Owner has full control • Very little financial reporting	• You have unlimited liability • You pay more tax (as soon as you earn enough to enter the higher-rate tax bracket) • Lacks credibility in market • Harder to get funding	Freelancers or low-cost businesses that are: • Not in need of funding (as soon as you are borrowing sums of money that could bankrupt you, you shouldn't be a sole trader) • Unlikely to earn more than the higher income tax thresholds	1. Register for self-assessment with HMRC 2. Complete annual tax return

TYPE	ADVANTAGES	DISADVANTAGES	BEST FOR...	NEXT STEPS
Partnership	• See above • Easier to get funding	• See above • Can be complex to terminate	Same as above, but for multiple individuals who are in business together. Often this structure is used for family businesses	1. Register your partnership for self-assessment with HMRC 2. Establish your partnership agreement 3. Each partner must submit an individual tax return
Limited company (LTD)	• Limited liability • Can be more tax efficient • Carries more credibility. The 'prestige' of being a company gives the impression that you have experience and can be trusted	• More administrative demands (directors must comply with Director's Fiduciary Responsibilities) • Annual accounts and financial reports are available publicly • Dividends don't qualify for pension relief	Businesses seeking funding and looking to scale	1. Register the limited company at Companies House 2. Submit annual accounts and a company tax return to HMRC each year 3. Pay employees' income tax and National Insurance

TYPE	ADVANTAGES	DISADVANTAGES	BEST FOR...	NEXT STEPS
Limited liability partnership (LLP)	• Flexibility over management roles, membership rights and profit distribution • Advantages of limited company and partnership combined	• Profit taxed as income • Partners must disclose income • LLP must start to trade within a year of registration – or be struck off • Expensive to set up	Businesses wanting a partnership model but with limited liability. Often used by professional services firms such as accountants	1. See points for limited company 2. Have an LLP agreement drawn up that says how the LLP will be run 3. Have at least two 'designated members'

Ultimately, it's down to you to weigh up the advantages and disadvantages of each structure and work out what's best suited to your business. It's a good idea to stick with the simplest structure that your business model will allow as you can always change to a different model once your business starts to scale. If in doubt, seek advice from an accountant who can advise you on the best course of action.

2. Branding

Successful businesses are far more than just the product or service they provide to customers. Just as people are unique, businesses also need their own identity to set them apart from the competition.

Brands help you achieve this by transporting the key messages of your business into the mind of a customer and helping it to stay there.

DO THIS > BUILD A BRAND

A helpful way to get started with your own brand is to imagine your business as a person. Ask questions like:

What are your values? E.g. resilience, wisdom, honesty	
What is your mission? E.g. to empower, entertain, comfort	
What is your personality? E.g. excitable, calm, effortless	
What is your tone of voice? E.g. youthful, professional, straight-talking	

Once you've conjured up a complete picture of your brand's personality, you can start to develop your brand identity. It's at this point that you may consider protecting your intellectual property. Every country will have its own rules, regulations and processes around this so it might be worth seeking legal advice. You may also choose to get some external help with your branding. Use the following diagram as a guide to ensure you've covered all bases:

SIX ESSENTIAL ELEMENTS OF A BRAND

3. Get equipped

Whilst some businesses might be operable from your laptop and sofa, others will require more substantial investment. Think about the resources and equipment that you might need to run your business. Outside of the cost of actually building your product or service, what are the initial outlays that you'll have to make?

As a rough guide, here are the kinds of set up costs that businesses usually face…

Resources and equipment checklist

- Technology – mobile phones, laptops, printers
- Online services – website and email hosting
- Stationery – office supplies
- Insurance – income insurance, employers' liability insurance, professional indemnity insurance
- Licences – appropriate licences to operate within a sector
- Branding – logo design, brand identity
- Office space – co-working space, managed office
- Legal/Accounting support – patenting, company registration, employment contracts

GFY + A NOTE ON… EXPENSES

One of the great advantages of being self-employed or running your own business is that you are able to deduct some of the costs of running your business from your income, which then makes up your taxable profit. The government sets out strict criteria as to what an 'allowable expense' is so make sure you check this before filing your expenses. There is no need to send proof of expenses when you submit your tax return, but make sure you keep copies so you can show them to HMRC if asked. It's also good practice to set aside some time each month to file your expenses. Don't let a tree's worth of receipts collect in the bottom of your bag – stay on top of them and you'll thank yourself by the time tax return season comes around. To make life even easier, there is also some great accounting software out there such as Xero, FreshBooks and FreeAgent, which allow you to snap a photo of a receipt, and file it via an app. We'll be looking at how to manage your business accounts in the next section.

4. Get online

In the digital age, there is a school of thought that if your business doesn't exist online, then is it even a business at all? For most businesses there is some truth in this, so before you launch make sure you've got your online identity nailed. The key to this is consistency; ensure that your brand and name is identical or, at the very least, highly similar across all the different platforms that you choose to exist on. Once you've chosen your name, use a username availability service to work out which names are already taken, claiming your own as quickly as possible. To make sure your business rises to the top of the search engine ranks, have a look at Search Engine Optimization (SEO) tools, which boost your rankings.

5. Organize your finances

The most important but possibly most yawn-inspiring aspect of running a business is getting a grip on your finances. We've already covered the basics of profits, revenue and cost, but you'll also need to find an effective way of managing your company's cash finances. Gone are the days of manual bookkeeping (unless that's what really floats your boat). Most businesses will either use their own accounting software, hire an accountant or use a bookkeeper. These can help track payments, monitor bills and basically do the hard stuff for you. However, whichever system you decide upon, it's still important to have a handle on how money is moving in and out of your business, and what that means for you.

Managing money in a business

1. Set up a business bank account

As a sole trader, technically you don't need to open a separate bank account, but, to save you getting into a financial mess, having separate business and personal bank accounts might be a good idea. Nearly all banks will be able to offer you a range of business accounts, so shop around to compare charges and offerings to get the best deal.

2. Managing your cash flow

Cash is oxygen to businesses: the faster you move, the more you need. In fact, cash is so essential to businesses, that, according to one study, 82 per cent of business failures can be blamed on poor cash flow management. Even if a business has enough assets to meet all of its liabilities in totality it is no good if they do not have enough liquid assets, such as cash, to be able to meet their current liabilities as and when they are due. This is what's known as being practically insolvent and will often result in creditors taking legal action against you, ultimately resulting in liquidation. It can also be illegal to trade whilst being practically insolvent and can have serious consequences for any director who does so.

- **Cash flow** – The money moving into and out of a business each month. When more money is going out than is coming in, a business has a cash flow issue.

You can envisage your business's cash flow as a cycle; in every business activity, from making new sales to paying suppliers, there are opportunities to be smart with your cash.

GFY + THE CASH FLOW CYCLE

Getting paid

- Send out invoices promptly
- Firmly chase debts
- Monitor paid and unpaid invoices

Making sales

- Use previous month's/year's data to forecast sales peaks and troughs. If you're in a seasonal market (e.g. ice cream), very careful planning is required to avoid becoming practically insolvent
- Stay on good terms with investors/lenders who might help you through difficult patches
- Re-evaluate pricing in relation to the economy and competitors but be sure not to undervalue yourself

Manage your cash in the business

- Use bookkeeping software and/ or an accountant
- Use previous month's/year's data to forecast and prepare for costs for the next month/year, setting cash aside for upcoming costs

Make payments

- Cut any unnecessary costs
- Compare suppliers and negotiate to get the best deal
- Negotiate the longest credit terms with suppliers and shortest payment terms with customers
- Consider whether you are making the most of tax-deductible expenses

Investing in your business/buying stock

- If you sell physical products, monitor your stock to work out what sells and what doesn't to ensure you're not left with redundant stock
- Be frugal, resist buying the latest equipment and fancy stationery

3. Keeping records

Keeping tidy financial records (called bookkeeping) might be the bane of many business owners' lives, but it's a necessity. Not only does the law require it, it's also a great way to check in on the health of your business. When it comes to bookkeeping, you've got two options: manual bookkeeping, where you produce and manage your financial statements on a spreadsheet; or electronic bookkeeping, where you use accounting software to automate your record keeping. For small one-person businesses, manual bookkeeping might suffice, but many find that accounting software saves them significant time.

Whichever you choose, these are three 'statements' that you need to know about:

- **Balance sheet** – Think of the balance sheet as a snapshot of everything your business owes (liabilities) and owns (assets) at a specific point in time. Assets include things such as cash, inventory and land, whereas liabilities include things such as unpaid loans and wages. Make sure your current liabilities (liabilities owed in the next year) can be covered by liquid assets (cash or an asset that can be readily converted to cash)

- **Income statement** – This shows how your business has performed from a profit or loss perspective, over a specific period of time. Think of the income statement as a funnel: starting at the top with income that the business has brought in, then gradually deducting all the costs and expenses that you've had to spend to make that money.

Depending on whether your revenue is greater than your costs, the 'bottom line' is the amount that you've either made in profit or loss

- **Cash flow statement** – Now you know all about good cash flow, it's time to get familiar with the cash flow statement! Rather than focusing on profit or loss, this statement simply looks at the inflow and outflow of cash over a specific period. This is vitally important for being able to forecast the cash coming in and also ensuring you have enough in the bank to pay your outgoings on time

4. Managing taxes

To end your immersion in the world of business finance on a high, let's look at taxes.

Unlike those in traditional employment, where your employer takes care of what you owe the taxman, those who are self-employed or run their own businesses need to be more proactive. Whilst it's tempting to adopt a 'head in the sand' approach, paying the right tax is important, and could save you from some nasty penalties. Given that taxes for the self-employed don't come straight out of your pay packet, you'll need to know what tax bills are coming up and set aside the cash in advance.

The table opposite covers the five taxes that you need to know about as a business owner and if/how they apply to sole traders and limited companies. For partnerships and LLPs, there are often much more complex tax arrangements so it's maybe worth seeking professional advice.

	SOLE TRADERS	LIMITED COMPANIES (LTD)
CORPORATION TAX	Not paid	Paid • a percentage of a business's profits or taxable income • Self-assessed and paid annually
VAT	Paid (if registered) • Paid by most businesses that sell products or services • Businesses whose revenue exceeds the VAT threshold must be registered for VAT • Charged as an additional fee on invoices and usually paid to HMRC quarterly • Businesses that are registered for VAT can claim back VAT on any purchases they make. If you aren't registered for VAT then VAT paid on purchases becomes a 'real cost'	
NATIONAL INSURANCE (NI)	Paid • Paid from their income by anyone earning more than the lower earnings limit (LEL)	Paid • Paid by employers on behalf of their employees • As the director of a company, you are also treated as an employee and must pay NI
INCOME TAX	Paid • Paid from the business's profits once they go above the 'personal allowance' • Must file a self-assessment form via HMRC	Paid • Paid on any salary you take from your business • Must file a self-assessment form via HMRC
BUSINESS RATES	Not paid	Paid • Paid by certain businesses usually those with designated premises

GFY + A WORD ON... PAYING THE TAXMAN

Each tax comes with its own protocol and procedure for paying it, with the thresholds and tax bands often changing. In the UK, HMRC's website provides clear instructions on how to pay your taxes and when. However, many find that a good accountant is money well spent. Not only will they help you with the logistics of submitting your tax return, they will also advise on ways to become more tax efficient.

Remember, whatever you choose to do, keep a close eye on tax deadlines, be proactive and set money aside to avoid any surprise tax bills or nasty penalties.

Make money, make a difference

'Greed is right, greed works... Greed, for lack of a better word, is good.' These are the words of banker Gordon Gecko in the 1987 film *Wall Street*. I like to think that in today's world, most of us find his attitude distasteful at best. Not pointing any fingers but it could be said that it's this same attitude that got us into the knee-trembling crisis of 2008. But we don't have to look far to see where this whole idea has come from. Flick through any microeconomics textbook and there you'll find one of the most fundamental principles of business: profit maximization – the assumption that businesses care most about their bottom line. In other words, make as much profit as possible, above all else.

But whilst economic theory may say one thing, in the three decades since the film was made, things have changed. If we were to invite Gordon back to a shareholder meeting today, I'm not sure his rallying cry would be met so favourably. As consumers we make careful choices about who we give our money to and what they do with it. We like companies that do good and can spot greedy ones a mile off.

In 2018 the CEO of Blackrock, the world's largest investment firm, got businesses thinking seriously about where their priorities lie:

Society is demanding that companies, both public and private, serve a social purpose. To prosper over time, every company must not only deliver financial performance, but also show how it makes a positive contribution to society.

In other words, this isn't just about ticking a 'socially responsible' box or slapping your logo on a charitable event. Having a mission, and purpose, which extends beyond the bottom line is vital to a business's survival. We want to see businesses doing good, serving communities better and creating products and services that maximize customer and social value, not just profit. The cynical may roll their eyes and claim that this kind of 'fluffy' activity is usually just off the back of a PR campaign but, regardless of the true motivation, there is no doubt that from the consumer's perspective this matters.

This has never been truer for the fashion business. In recent years, research has shone light on the saddening truths behind our love of 'fast fashion' and its impact on the environment. In 2017, a report by the Ellen MacArthur Foundation found that, if current rates continue, the global fashion industry could use more than a quarter of the world's annual carbon budget by 2050. It's not just the manufacturing processes that are unsustainable. With affordability comes disposability; in 2017 alone, over 300,000 tonnes of clothing ended up in landfill. There is a general consensus that something has to change.

Where many businesses see these statistics and calls to action as a threat, others see opportunity. Outerwear brand Patagonia is one of a handful of companies which are putting responsible manufacturing and consumption at the heart of their business. Since they opened in 1983, they've committed to donating a portion of their sales to non-profit environmental causes, totalling a staggering $185 million. But perhaps the most radical example of Patagonia's mission was their 'Don't Buy This Jacket' campaign. Coinciding with the annual consumer buying frenzy that is Black Friday, the ad urged shoppers to reuse and re-wear clothes they already had, as opposed to buying new. This kind of activity would be viewed as retail suicide by many high street brands, but for Patagonia their financials have never been stronger. In the past five years they've seen a tripling of profits with the company now valued at over a billion dollars.

There's no doubt that the principles of making money and making a difference are becoming increasingly interwoven. A social entrepreneur is the term for a person who establishes an enterprise with the aim of solving social problems or effecting social change, a choice that now carries weight in the world of business. It's also becoming easier or more accepted for businesses to bypass the traditional business principles of profit maximization. The growing 'B Corporation' movement frees corporations from their legal requirement to deliver maximum returns for shareholders, meaning they can pursue their social or environmental mission more effectively.

On the side

From the likes of Sophia Amoruso, who started her multi-million-dollar clothing line Nasty Gal from her college bedroom, to Adam Neumann, who founded WeWork after renting out some empty desks in his office, today's side projects could be tomorrow's greatest businesses. In recent years, the term 'side hustle' has crept into our vocabularies, defining and validating our growing interest in starting businesses in our spare time. One study revealed that over a third of sixteen- to thirty-four-year-olds have a money-making project alongside their full-time job.

However, it's not all bedroom billionaires and IPOs. Whilst the side hustle might be a stepping stone to financial freedom for some, it's a 'second job' undergone a glamourous rebrand for others. Working on the side can be a necessity: an unfortunate symptom of the ever-narrowing gap between our living costs and incomes. It's not always about being entrepreneurial or achieving your life goals, it's about making ends meet in a world of zero-hour contracts, high living costs and low wages. It might also be something in between. Maybe you're happy with your main earner but want to pad out your income with some extra cash to supplement your travels or simply gain some additional experience that you wouldn't otherwise get through your day job.

There is a whole spectrum of motivations for starting something but, whatever your reason, side businesses can be a great way to dip your toes into the entrepreneurial waters, without taking on all the risks of diving in head first. That's not to say it's all plain sailing. Juggling your main gig and something on the side requires bucket loads of self-motivation, time and a willingness to try and fail on a daily basis. So, if you think the side hustle approach might be right for you, here are five things to consider:

1. Validate

Whether you're running your business on the side or it's your full-time gig, validating your business idea should be your number one. If you've skipped straight to this section, go back to 'How to validate your ideas' on pp. 88–99 and then we can talk…

2. Create more time

It's a no brainer: in sticking to your day job whilst also establishing a business on the side, a lack of time can quickly become your most challenging obstacle. To find more, you're going to have to assess how you spend it. Run an audit of your weekly routine and select your 'non-negotiables', things you just can't cut and the things that you can probably do without (at least for now). Cancelling your Netflix subscription or blocking social media access might sound hardcore, but you'd be amazed how much time disappears into the sink holes of the internet without you realizing. Finally, just like you would when meeting a friend, schedule in daily or weekly time with yourself to work on your business and, most importantly, do it.

3. Set goals

Entrepreneurs set their sights high, whether it's wanting to become no. 1 in their niche or to be valued at over a billion in five years' time. However, when the going gets tough, it's the smaller, more achievable goals that will pull you through the dark times and keep you on track. Although eyes may roll at yet another cringey acronym, 'SMART' could be a helpful framework for thinking about your goals, making sure they are Specific, Measurable, Achievable, Relevant, and Time-bound.

Equally, having a purpose behind these goals is just as important. In step 1 of the Money Plan, we talked about the power of 'Why': not only knowing what you want to achieve but also *why* you want to achieve it. This means thinking about both your personal motivations for doing this and also the impact you want to have on the world too.

4. Don't get fired

You're working on the side for a good reason: most likely because you want to keep your full-time job, for now at the very least. As tempting as it might be to send out a cheeky email on company time or use their resources to help further your business, you could end up in dangerous waters. To avoid any nasty disputes, or even legal proceedings, be sure to check your employment contract for rules around non-competition or having another project or job on the side. You don't just want to avoid conflict with your employer, you want to stay on great terms too. You never know how they might be able to help you out down the road, be it connecting you to their network, or perhaps even allowing you to take unpaid leave to pursue your business.

5. Quit carefully

If your ultimate dream is to hand in your notice and fly solo, take some time to figure out how you're going to make the leap safely. Assuming you've already validated your business and already have paying customers, there are two factors you should consider before taking the plunge:

- **Business finances** – Either you have received funding for your business which will cover your costs for twelve months, or, if you're bootstrapping, your business should already have a steady cash flow which covers its own costs.
- **Personal finances** – You should have either saved or fundraised enough money to cover your personal expenses for at least six months (see pp. 152–60 on how to calculate this) or, if your business is generating enough to cover these, make sure you have an emergency fund to tide you over in case things don't go to plan.

A(nother) word on failure

Success is not final, failure is not fatal: it is the courage to continue that counts.

Winston Churchill

You are going to fail. Whether it's this business or the next. At work. In your relationships. Failure is a part of life. But what society doesn't tell us is that failure is also a part of success. In an interview at the World Economic Forum, billionaire Jack Ma recounted his numerous failures: from not getting a job in KFC, even though twenty-three out of twenty-four applicants were hired, to being rejected by Harvard ten times. These failures weren't unfortunate instances that happened before he was successful, they propelled him towards success. He explains: 'If you don't give up, you still have a chance. Giving up is the greatest failure.'

Fear of failure is inbuilt. Remember the internal caveman we talked about in 'Earn it'? Well, he's back and this time he's freaking out. If switching careers sent him into flat spin, you can only imagine the kind of state starting a business would get him into. He's not just worried about the practical consequences; how you'll feed yourself and pay the rent, but the social ones too. What will the tribe say when it all goes wrong? Won't I be a total outcast? It's just too embarrassing to even think about. To rein in our wild ambitions and keep us on the straight and narrow, we've evolved to be inherently loss averse, meaning we'll go to far greater lengths to avoid failure than we will to achieve success.

So how do we talk ourselves into thinking more optimistically? Rather than let our brains catastrophize all that could go wrong in taking action, we need to take a balanced view and consider the alternative. What would happen if you *didn't* give this a go? How would life look in two, five or ten years' time? Would you regret this? What would life look like if it were a success?

Of course, there is a possibility that your plans won't work out. When it comes to starting a business, there are always going to be variables beyond your control which could spell failure. As you might expect, first-time entrepreneurs have a higher rate of failure than those who have started a business before, but that shouldn't put you off. In fact, many of the world's most successful entrepreneurs have not only started businesses but failed at them too. Reid Hoffman, founder of LinkedIn, James Dyson of Dyson Vacuums and Nicholas Woodman, founder of GoPro, all had failed businesses before launching their, now billion-dollar, companies. Whilst nobody wishes for failure, it's often the training ground for later success. Invest time, with good intention, into anything you believe in and you will always get something back. It might not be in the shape or size that you originally anticipated, but you will be rewarded in one way or another.

However, it's also important to remember that there is nothing wrong with giving up and moving on. Whilst at one point you might have felt that entrepreneurship is for you, it's OK if that's no longer the case. The very experience of having tried something that you believed in is not only an incredibly valuable learning process, it's a credit to your character. As businesses are forced to adapt, employers are increasingly on the lookout for entrepreneurial talent who think outside the box. So, if your concern is employability, cast those fears aside.

The process of starting a business is a bit like skydiving. Whilst the strategies outlined in this chapter will make the dive less likely to end in complete disaster, the jumping is down to you. Whilst reading, analysing and strategizing will go some way to making you feel more prepared, starting a business will always require blind faith. You will never feel comfortable, so there comes a time when you have to make a choice:

- Act on it
- Set it free

You either act on ideas or you set them free. You don't dwell on ideas.

Casey Neistat

PART IV

SPEND IT

PART 1:
HOW WE SPEND IT TODAY

The case of Anna Delvey

In February 2017, Anna Delvey moved to New York. Daughter of a business magnate and inheritor of a sizeable trust fund, Anna quickly assumed the title of New York's latest 'it girl'. She was the epitome of Manhattan chic: flitting from party, to Michelin restaurant, to fortnightly European city break. Whispers that she'd flown in by private jet, papped in the company of celebrities such as Macaulay Culkin, not to mention how she'd indulge her friends with extravagant gifts, only proved to sceptics that she must be the real deal.

However, the Anna Delvey that New York had come to know was a fake; a cleverly curated disguise of Anna Sorokin, a Russian born and German raised, run-of-the-mill girl, who'd spent a couple of years interning at a fashion magazine. Fabricating her own financial advisor, under the not so elaborate front of an AOL email address, she was able to convince bank representatives to extend her a line of credit that would go on to fund her excessive lifestyle and convince her socialite circles that she was legit. This, followed by a couple of bad cheques, allowed her to rack up unpaid bills upwards of $275,000. As with all good tales of fraud and deception, it didn't end well for Anna. The unpaid bills weren't going to pay themselves, so it wasn't long before her cover was blown. In October 2017 she was indicted on grand larceny charges and now faces four to twelve years in jail.

The story of Anna is the *Catch Me If You Can* of the internet age. Although, unlike the fraudsters of yesteryear, Anna wasn't the mastermind of some sort of elaborate Ponzi scheme. Nor was she the criminal behind a complex case of identity fraud. Anna simply took advantage of a bias that we're all capable of falling victim to: the belief that wealth is what we see. Not only that, we like what we see too. With the mere flash of a platinum Amex, and a flick of an expensive blow dry, she had Manhattan eating from the palm of her hand. Her front was hardly watertight. A 'German heiress' that couldn't speak German?! But what did that matter? She wore the right clothes, knew the right people and attended the right parties, all meticulously documented on her Instagram. Nobody questioned what lay beneath.

Anyone with so much as a thumb on social media will be proficient in the art of 'self-curation': hand picking the moments of our lives that present our most enviable self, leaving the bad and ugly bits lurking on our camera roll. However, Anna took this a step further. She wasn't in the business of 'curation', but full-blown manufacturing. Not only did she create her identity online, she quite literally brought it to life. What is usually confined to the 2:2 square of an Instagram post, she gave a heartbeat, making the case for her authenticity only stronger. Anna's story is an extreme one but, nonetheless, it's a fascinating insight into our willingness to believe what we see. Maybe we're more vulnerable to deception but I think there's a part of us that wants to believe it could all be true. Maybe, just maybe, we could do it too.

Creating illusions of wealth has also become big business. In January 2016, the following headline made mainstream press: 'University dropout becomes a stockbroker after using his student loan to start trading and now claims he earns £30,000 on a BAD month.' The story details how one young Londoner amassed a small fortune by working 'just one hour a day', from the comfort of his own home. Look at his social channels and you'll find a stream of cliched images, from wads of cash in briefcases to private jet selfies. It's no surprise that he and the hundreds of other so-called 'trader millionaires' have garnered an almost heroic status within their own internet subculture, encouraging kids with ambitions of wealth and success to join the trader fray. Yet in reality, their supposed 'fortune' is much less thanks to trading and much more down to their convincing sales patter. Operating on behalf of trading platforms and other highly risky financial products, they're selling the promise of wealth and in exchange, cashing in on sizeable commission fees. Flaunting their riches under hashtags such as #binaryoptions (222,206), #traderlifestyle (64,151) and #richkidsofinstagram (529,574), they're the poster boys of financial aspiration and success. DM for their latest trading strategy and you too could be standing at the foot of your very own jet with a pair of Yeezy's in every colourway. The real tragedy of these schemes lies in the disappointment and, in some cases, serious financial loss of those who had hopes of building wealth. And, more often than not, it's the most vulnerable who fall victim: young people with ambition but without access to prestigious city careers.

For younger generations who feel hopeless about their financial futures, it's a worry that a simple Instagram account is capable of creating such a compelling, yet totally fraudulent, promise.

But it's not just celebrities and the Insta-famous that we need to look out for. In one way or another, we're all a bit guilty of peddling some illusion that life is just a little richer than it actually is. And it's the reality of our financial predicament that is the first to be filtered out. We post the beach holiday pic, not the embarrassment of having to tell our friend that we couldn't afford the really cool Airbnb that they could. We post the bottomless brunch, not the anxiety we felt as it sent us into overdraft. We post our promotion, not the year spent as an unpaid intern. Taking aim at the soaring heights of 'Insta goals', firing our rigorously examined and edited snaps up into the social media ether, we're all doing our bit to push the benchmarks of success, wealth and happiness even higher.

Open up

Adopting a healthy dose of scepticism when it comes to the 'wealth' we see is one positive step we can make towards managing our own money better. But what about our own spending? What would happen if we made a conscious effort to be just a little more open about our financial realities? Younger generations are proving that it's OK to be vulnerable with money, with them feeling more comfortable talking to a friend about what they earn than older generations. We're also deeply curious when it comes to what other people earn and do with their cash. Refinery29's 'Money Diaries' series has taken the internet by storm, documenting the salaries and spending habits of young women across the globe. We love to peruse the financial virtues and vices of people like us.

But this kind of openness isn't just a source of lunchbreak amusement. There is power in divulging both our successes and struggles with money. Because the fact is, financial pride comes at a very literal cost. Preserving an image of financial cool and hiding the truths that lurk inside our own wallets is an expensive business. Since I started writing this book, friends have admitted that they too frequently spend money, not out of wanting to but out of feelings of obligation or pressure. Whether it's buying a new outfit for that wedding as opposed to reusing the one you wore last month, or saying no to eating out at that hideously expensive restaurant, many of us struggle to be vulnerable with our finances.

Case in point, I recently went on a date with a guy who suggested we meet at his favourite wine bar. 'What a cute place,' I thought for about two seconds, before noticing that the cheapest bottle was £40. 'Let's go for this one,' he said, gesturing at a Chilean red uncomfortably far down the menu. I gulped. 'Shall we get a charcuterie board too?' he asked himself briefly, before confirming to the waiter that, 'Yes, we'll have one of those.' I knew we'd be splitting the bill and I knew that I definitely couldn't afford the £75 that had racked up in the first ten minutes of meeting him. 'Sorry, do you mind if we go for a different one? I'm on a tight budget this month,' is what I should have said, but didn't. Instead, I smiled as I calculated the pound-per-sip of the apparently delicious 'New World Cabernet Sauvignon' that was about to be served.

Saying no takes a certain kind of confidence and it is needed in even higher doses when it means baring all financially. If we dig beneath our financial pride, it's often quite a different emotion that holds us back: shame. An emotion which, according to scholar Brené Brown, needs three things to grow exponentially in our lives: secrecy, silence and judgement. A triple threat when it comes to our finances. It's by sweeping our money worries under the carpet that our shame is compounded, making us more anxious and less in control.

Openness doesn't just make for better financial decision making. Honesty punctures the Instagram bubble that we're all guilty of inflating, helping us to feel a little better about the boat that, inevitably, we're all in. Sharing truths, be it worry over debt, frustration over unequal pay or curiosity about investing, can also be a great source of knowledge and, in turn, power, ultimately giving you the confidence to take control of your money.

However, the challenge of this kind of thinking is that it forces us to tap out of the game that humans have been playing for millennia. To a greater or lesser degree, we all have a desire to 'keep up with the Joneses'. A game so prolific that it's even inspired the reality show of Instagram's most famous family. With today's 'If you didn't post it, did it even happen?!' mentality, the stakes are even higher. 'Keeping up' is both an offline and online business.

In a first-world capitalist society where, in theory, everything is up for grabs, it's natural to want to present our successes to the world. And with money often one of the most tangible manifestations of success, spending it on 'things' is a normal expression, even a celebration, of our achievements. And I'm all for celebrating. Just as wanting to make loads of money is a worthy ambition so long as that's what makes you feel great, the same goes for spending it. Money shouldn't be wrapped up in shame, and, as such, we shouldn't shame anyone else for how they choose to spend it. You do you. The danger, however, is when our motivations for both wanting it and spending it become not about serving ourselves but rather a means to 'keep up'.

The irony is that when it comes to possessions, most people aren't interested in what you have. Despite efforts to make conspicuous displays of wealth, it's more often than not in vain. The Rich Man in the Car paradox explains how whilst the owner of a new lambo might want you to think, 'Wow. Look how cool he is in that ridiculously expensive car,' what we tend to think is, 'Wow. Imagine how cool I would look in a car like that,' or possibly: 'What a k**b'. We're all in our own heads, too busy creating our own benchmarks of wealth and success, to be worried about you or your money.

What does money look like?

It's not that we need to become better at working out who's got the cash and who hasn't. In fact, it's not about making judgements at all. Real money is invisible but, with all the secrecy and pride we've talked about, we just don't see into other people's financial situations. However, being the curious creatures that we are, our brain finds ways to make its own conclusions. Short of sneaking onto someone's banking app, or Googling the value of their house, we draw on the best reference point we have: stuff. Eyeing up the owner of a £100,000 Ferrari, we conclude they *must* be stupidly rich to be able to spend so much money on something like a car. And they might be, but you don't *know* that. All you know is that they have £100,000 less than before they bought the car. With credit virtually on tap, you don't even know if the car is theirs at all. The truth is, real money is what you don't see. It's the car that wasn't bought. The Gucci belt left on the shelf. The bonus unspent. When Rihanna accused her financial advisor of not preventing her from nearing bankruptcy, he responded: 'Was it really necessary to tell her that if you spend money on things, you will end up with the things and not the money?' It sounds so ridiculously obvious, but the truth is, yes… sometimes we do. When I say, 'I want to be a millionaire,' what I probably mean is, 'I would really like to spend a million pounds.'

Spending isn't buying

Having things has never been so easy, which makes understanding the difference between having things and having money even more important. Year on year, consumer debt has been rising and, for the first time in nearly thirty years, 2017 saw UK households' annual outgoings surpass their income. In other words, we're buying things with money we don't have. Over the past five years, borrowing on all fronts from loans, credit cards, overdrafts and second mortgages has soared, with the National Audit Office estimating that 8.3 million people in the UK are unable to pay off their debts or keep on top of household bills. In many cases, getting into debt isn't a choice; with shrinking disposable incomes, debt is a necessary last resort and, unsurprisingly, it's the least wealthy that are most affected. In 2017, the poorest 10 per cent of households spent, on average, two and a half times their disposable income, whilst the richest 10 per cent spent less than half.

At the same time, the temptation to live beyond our means has never been so great.

With interest rates at all-time lows, buying 'on finance' has become both increasingly alluring and available. Have a terrible credit rating? Eating into your overdraft every month? Unable to save a penny due to stupidly high rents? Worry not, welcome to the world of credit, where a Rolex, a holiday to St Barth's and a kitchen renovation can all be yours with a digestible monthly payment plan and no upfront cost. With what have been criticized as fairly superficial affordability checks, yesterday's luxuries, only purchased after months, if not years, of saving, can now be yours within minutes. The patience that was once required to save up for expensive items is now redundant. Although buying credit might feel like a shortcut to living your #bestlife, with the phones, cars and watches to boot, the reality is spending and owning are two very different things.

Low interest rates have played their part in making debt more appealing, but the past few decades have seen a shift in our perceptions of debt too. Throughout the ages, debt and its connotations with wealth and class have swung from one extreme to the other. During the 18th and 19th centuries, debt was a luxury; a symbol of status afforded only by the wealthy as a means of buying the necessary trappings of an upper-class lifestyle. At the time, half of all heads of household died leaving outstanding debts. It wasn't for people who couldn't afford things, but rather used by people who *could* afford it. The attitude of the time is captured in the questionable advice of notorious spender Oscar Wilde, who remarked:

> *Anyone who lives within their means suffers from a lack of imagination.*

Despite coming from relative wealth, by the age of twenty-two Oscar had racked up significant debts, with one bank statement detailing a particularly expensive splurge on a 'fancy Angora suit'.

But as the banking industry scaled throughout the 20th century, access to credit reached the mass market. One example was the Tallyman of the early 20th century: a travelling sales-man who would knock on doors selling household goods in exchange for a weekly payment. Gone were the days of debt be-ing a facility preserved only for the wealthy, quite the opposite. However, up until the 1950s, being able to manage your finances properly was a source of enormous pride, so the need to borrow just wasn't talked about.

It was only in the latter part of the 20th century and into the 21st that innovations made debt both more accessible and acceptable. TV advertising was a major catalyst: a door to a whole new world of the latest fashions and must have gadgets.

The key came in the form of mail order catalogues, credit cards, re-mortgaging and, more recently, online loans. All of which opened up an entirely new financial paradigm. It wasn't long before the desire to 'have' overrode any of the pre-existing stigmas or judgments.

And things are shifting once again. The 'sharing economy' has exploded into existence with the likes of Airbnb, Zipcar and Spotify paving the way for a generation of consumers who would rather just access goods or services when they need them, rather than owning them. The brilliance of all these innovations can't be denied, with them offering better value and access to the end consumer. But, at the same time, it's both interesting and important to be conscious of how our perceptions of owning, having and spending are being radically reshaped once again.

More is better

Wanting less is a better blessing than having more.

Mary Ellen Edmunds

The idea that having more stuff is a prerequisite to being happy or successful lies at the heart of consumerism, which is one of the strongest influences on how we spend money. On an average day, we're exposed to over 1,600 commercial messages; that's cash 1,600 companies have spent in order to dangle their wares before your eyes, usually touting the message that in one way or another 'your life could be better if...' In the 2012 James Bond film *Skyfall*, Sony, Belvedere, Bollinger, Heineken and Omega all paid multi-million-pound sums to claim their place as the agent's brand of choice. Although we're all wise to the prolific use of product placement and advertising more broadly, consumerism is so much more than these things – it is what underpins our entire understanding of economic success. Before the Second World War the term 'consumer' had nothing to do with buying. People purchased the things they needed, they didn't 'consume' them. It was only in the thirties, America's post-Depression era, when governments and marketers were set a challenge: to think creatively about how they could get more money into the economy.

By pushing the idea that consumerism equated 'The American Way', citizens were persuaded to pursue 'more, newer and better', an ideology endorsed by economist Viktor Lebow who famously proclaimed that: 'We need things consumed, burned up, worn out, replaced and discarded at an ever-increasing rate.' It's a sentiment that today sounds horrifying, but back then consumerism was rationalized, not only as a means for individuals to achieve the glorious ideal of 'The American Dream', but also as a tool for economic growth. If people consumed more, the economy would grow more too. The idea was soon made global by the adoption of GDP as the main measure of economic success; a metric that is quite literally founded on the principle that 'more spending = more prosperous'.

Today, however, this philosophy is starting to jar with all we know about the damage that consumerism inflicts on both the environment and our psychology. Because as we consume more, we waste more too. Ever heard of 'The Great Pacific

Garbage Patch'? Google it. And even those who manage to achieve contentment with what they have face a practical challenge. For fear of sounding like my grandmother, things just aren't built to last these days. Manufacturers have found ways to ensure that what we have now won't satisfy us for long. Planned product obsolescence is the practice of building products that have a deliberately shortened lifespan. Cheeky right? Think back to university or school where you'd be urged to buy the latest edition of a textbook, even though it bore almost identical resemblance to the previous thirty-two. Or your smartphone, with an irreplaceable lithium-ion battery that suspiciously decreases in performance just as the latest model is released. But perhaps the industry most guilty of peddling a culture of disposability is 'fast fashion'; retailers manufacturing inexpensive, 'on trend' designs that move quickly from the catwalk to stores. Once upon a time, there were two seasons in the fashion world: Spring/Summer and Autumn/Winter. Now we have fifty-two. A non-stop pipeline of 'micro seasons', with new pieces delivered into stores and online each week. Not only has this upped the pace at which we need to 'keep up' but, as we talked about it in 'Start it', it's also having a detrimental impact on our environment, with fashion now the second largest polluter, just behind oil.

Our ferocious appetite for having more 'stuff' doesn't just exist on a social level, but on a neurobiological one too. In many ways, we're our own victims. In 2007, researchers from MIT, Stanford University and Carnegie Mellon University explored the neurological effects of shopping. Using fMRI scanners, they found that buying things stimulated the 'pleasure centre' of the brain just in the same way that sex and chocolate would. You might expect that, but the experiment didn't only find a connection between shopping and pleasure, but pain too. When looking at how our brain responds to price, they discovered that a high price tag has a near identical effect to that of a physical injury in activating our pain centres. Interestingly, shopping on a credit card effectively anaesthetized the pain associated with purchasing, perhaps another explanation for our love of credit and the growing debt crisis.

Many things are cheaper too. Items that were once luxuries, purchased only by the wealthiest and most privileged, have been commoditized, largely thanks to advances in manufacturing techniques, better communications and globalization. Take TVs for example. In the fifties, a television set would have set you back around £248 (£6,400 in today's money), accounting for over 80 per cent of an average salary. By comparison, today this figure is less than 3 per cent.

However, our appetites are changing. Over the past decade, mounting awareness of the connection between how we spend our money and its wider implications has begun to translate into good news. In the UK, recycling rates are on the up and less waste is being sent to landfill. The 'slow fashion movement' is a tangible example of our changing behaviour which has rallied consumers across the world to purchase good quality, environmentally clean and fairly produced clothing. We're also seeing a cultural shift in attitudes to consumerism. For example, when Macklemore released 'Thrift Shop' during my first year at university, I definitely wasn't thinking about its social significance. It was just that song that enticed

WKD-drowned eighteen-year-olds onto the sticky club floor. To the credit of Macklemore, the song is actually more profound than our student selves could have ever realized; what we were listening to was in fact a powerful critique of the usual displays of wealth and excess associated with hip hop music videos. 'Rappers talk about, oh I buy this and I buy that, and I spend this much money and I make it rain, and this type of champagne and painting the club,' Macklemore explains. 'It's the polar opposite of it. It's kind of standing for, like, let's save some money, let's keep some money away, let's spend as little as possible and look as fresh as possible at the same time.' Amen, Macklemore.

The (un)true value of money

We don't just use money as an exchange for things such as clothes, food or entertainment. We also exchange it for ourselves. What we earn is our market valuation; a sum total of our skills and experiences. A reflection of how much someone is willing to pay for us. Or so traditional economic theory would say. It sounds brutal, right? We don't like being reduced to a single figure and know that, obviously, we're worth so much more than just a paycheck. The offence we take at the idea of being some kind of workplace commodity isn't just rooted in the belief that we are more than just money but because money is so much more than just a number. Beyond what it can buy, money has a secondary value; not in the quantitative sense that we can all agree on but a personal and highly subjective symbolic value. As we grow up and become increasingly exposed to the concepts of wealth, finance, rich and poor, we internalize our own theories as to what we think money means. Theories that vary wildly from person to person and sit somewhere on a spectrum from money holding a huge emotional weight to seeing it purely as a tool.

To a greater or lesser degree, we all see money through an emotional lens. For you it might be: power, success or freedom; for someone else: fear, evil or control. The reason that it's so important to understand the emotional value that *you* give money is that it shapes not only how you think about it but how you spend, save, invest, give and earn it too. I know this might sound like a pile of psycho-waffle but hear me out, there is some actual science behind it all. You see, research has found that when we think about money as an emotional end in itself, it tends to make it much more challenging to manage.

The figure in our bank account starts to feel like an extension of us, shaping how we feel about ourselves and, at a social level, shaping how we feel about other people. Emotional baggage applies to your finances too! If you believe that money IS success or that money IS freedom, then how much you earn will directly affect whether you feel you have either of those things; your self-worth becomes dictated by your bank balance. Not good. By extension, this attitude also impacts how we feel about others who have more or less money than we do. For example, in the case of success, you might perceive a friend with a higher salary to be more successful than you, probably leading to serious discontentment, comparison and jealousy. This kind of thinking sets an infinite benchmark for our happiness; more will always be better and as such we will never have enough.

Perhaps the most significant effect of this kind of thinking is what it means for how we actually manage and earn our money. Because what we think drives our behaviours, it goes without saying that emotional thinking will often lead to emotional decisions. When money spells success then, of course, you'd choose the highest-paying job. If money is best when saved and not spent, then we'll feel reluctant and stressed about letting it go. If we believe that it's the root of all evil, we may give in to its perceived 'power' and accept that we just don't have the ability to control our spending or reach our financial goals.

The research is clear: people who think about money purely in its practical terms, as an instrument, find money management easier. They're likely to have less debt, more savings and lower levels of financial stress. On the other hand, when we start to think about money emotionally we're likely to be more anxious, have lower self-esteem and more financial fear. But there's a catch-22: those who have less money in the first place are more likely to tie it up with emotional values. It's easy to see how vicious cycles can emerge: a low income might lead to financial stress, compounded by unhelpful emotional beliefs, in turn making its management even harder, and creating even more financial worry. It's a minefield that can seem impossible to escape and it's why simply urging someone to just 'be better' at money is pointless. Most of the time, we have to lift the lid on our spending and look at what really goes on.

DO THIS > IDENTIFY YOUR FINANCIAL MINDSET

If your eyes are rolling right now then maybe you've nailed your financial mindset. But if any of it rings true, understanding your own might be a helpful move towards being better with money.

Ask yourself the following questions without using any money-related words (rich, poor, wealthy, broke etc.)

1. Having more money than anyone I know motivates me
    → Yes
    → No (go to 3)
2. Why would having more money than anyone you know be a good thing?
3. a) When you discover someone has significantly more money than you what do you think about them?
    b) What does it make you think about yourself?
4. If I had more money I would feel...
5. If I had less money I would feel...
6. When I pay a bill I feel...
7. When I get a unexpected windfall of money, I feel...

Looking over your answers, what are the common beliefs or themes that pop up?

So how do we break the cycle and think about money, better? First, you need to see money for what it actually is: a tool that *you* have control over. It isn't love, success, freedom or any other feeling or emotion. And it's not a reflection of who you are or what you're worth. Money is inherently neutral. Just as a brick can be used to both build a house and break a window, the value of money is not in what we feel about it but in what we do with it. Money can help achieve happiness just as it can bring misery. You can be happy and rich, just as you can be happy and poor. Money can come with success, but having it doesn't mean you are successful. It can be used for evil just as it can for good.

It's not that we need to cast all our money worries aside, give it all away or join a commune. Money is absolutely necessary to meet your human needs and wants, but that is exactly the point: it's a tool that meets our needs, not a need in itself. Simply 'having' money is totally useless; you could have millions tucked away your whole life but without the ability to spend it, what good is it?!

So, to think about money and manage it better, with less stress, we need to untangle it from the emotional crap that it has become caught up in. Crap which (to get a little Freudian) has probably been shaped during our early life. While I was writing this book, for example, one friend told me about the impact of the credit crisis on her family: 'After my dad was made redundant, our family lifestyle underwent a massive shift… we couldn't afford the holidays and I saw the tension it created between my mum and dad. It sounds bad but I guess money was something which made my mum feel good about herself and proud. When we had less, it really dented her confidence and status... I've definitely picked up some of those beliefs.' Another spoke about how attending a prestigious boarding school on a full scholarship had shaped her own ideas around money: 'I always had less. My family couldn't afford the school trips, the music lessons or the extra tutoring. Money has always been an obstacle... something that stands between me and what I want to achieve.' Another spoke about her family's extreme scrimping and saving: 'Money was always an object of stress... something that needed to be controlled and constantly managed before anything else. Now, just thinking about my bank balance makes me anxious... so I've definitely gone the other way and have a "head in the sand" attitude to money.'

DO THIS > FIX YOUR FINANCIAL MINDSET

So, once you've decided to see money as a tool you can acknowledge that more or less of it can't make you anything more or less than you are now. Emotional beliefs around money aren't a reflection of what money actually is but much more a reflection of what we believe we're lacking. Looking over your answers from 'Identify your money mindset', ask yourself what lies beneath your feelings about money? Is there anything you think you aren't or don't have?

Below is just an example of what different feelings *could* mean:

Beliefs		Meaning
Power	→	Lack of control
Status	→	Lack of self-confidence
Guilt	→	Lack of permission or acceptance
Happiness	→	Lack of contentment
Regret	→	Lack of self-compassion
Shame	→	Lack of self-trust

In whatever way you think money might make you feel good or bad, it really won't, but the challenge is that when you haven't yet 'made it' this can seem impossible to believe. In the brilliant words of Jim Carrey:

'I wish people could realize all their dreams and wealth and fame so they could see it's not where you're going to find your sense of completion... there is nothing bigger than yourself.'

PART 2:
THE 'SPENDING' IT ESSENTIALS

We've covered all the fun bits which hopefully means you've got a handle on all the external forces which make money management hard and also have a better understanding of how *you* think about your own money. Now being good at it becomes a whole lot easier. This is where the spending it essentials come in; the simple and proven methods to help you budget, get out of debt and 'do money' better.

Budget better, spend better

The bad news is, yes, you do need a budget; the good news? I'm going to show you a method which won't take years to get your head around or require you to go anywhere near Microsoft Excel.

But why? Why on earth do we have to put ourselves through something so tedious, time consuming and, well, let's be honest, unsexy? What is the point? Well, the basic principle of a budget is simple: INCOME > SPENDING

The 50:30:20 method

Rather than set yourself the mind-numbing, not to mention unachievable, challenge of creating a budget for various types of expenditure, the 50:30:20 technique is budgeting at its simplest. The general principle is that by breaking down your income into three categories, you can set yourself clear spending targets, give yourself a little freedom, whilst also prioritizing your long-term goals. The three categories and ideal* percentages are:

- **Needs** (50 per cent): e.g. Rent, groceries, tax (if you're self-employed)
- **Wants** (30 per cent): e.g. Netflix subscription, holidays, overpriced flat whites
- **Goals** (20 per cent): e.g. Paying off debts, saving for your long-term future

So how does it work in practice?

Step 1: Calculate your post-tax income

If you're an employee with a steady paycheque, your after-tax income should be easy to figure out: it's what remains after taxes, student loan repayments and pension contributions have been deducted. Basically, whatever lands in your current account each month. If you're self-employed, you'll need to set aside money for tax and contribute to your own pension first.

Step 2: What are you actually spending?

Knowledge is power, so first things first, let's work out where your money is actually going. Spoiler: it's probably on food and rent. Thankfully, it has never been easier to track your cash. With budgeting and banking apps that helpfully categorize your expenditure, gone are the days of old-school receipt keeping and Excel spreadsheets (although if that works, you do you). Find an app or method that gives you a simple and clear view of your spending habits.

DO THIS > WHAT ARE YOU SPENDING?

- Take your last three months of spending and separate your wants from your needs. You can either do this on a transaction by transaction basis or save time and categorize transactions (e.g. eating out -> want, utilities -> need). There are plenty of great 'read only' open-banking apps that can help you with this (see gofundyourself.co).
- Work out your average monthly spend in each category and its % of your post-tax income.

Monthly post-tax income _____

	Monthly spending (£)	% of monthly post-tax income
NEEDS		
WANTS		
GOALS		

GFY + DEFINING WANTS AND NEEDS

The 50:30:20 is no different from most philosophies and techniques concerning budgeting: separating wants from needs as a way of enforcing self-control around spending. But I think we need to redefine 'need'. I promised from the outset that there would be no mention of what you should and shouldn't spend your money on. Who am I to tell you to cut back on coffee or take the bus?! Rather than prescribed ideas about what can be justified as a 'need', I think we need to inject a little more generosity into our narratives around our personal finance. There's a risk that in separating all spending that doesn't fall into the 'food/shelter/would die without' category, we make our finances so much more stressful than they need to be. Sure, that delicious cinnamon bun that you treat yourself to every weekend might not be critical to your existence but maybe it's that little treat that fights off the Sunday blues. What might be a total extravagance for one, might be a necessity for another and that's OK. Nothing is black and white, money included. Just as a healthy relationship with food isn't about restriction, but rather balance, we need to adopt a similar approach to our spending. Move away from seeing spending in such binary terms: from good and bad to a healthier, more balanced, mindset.

Step 3: What is your ideal spending?

Based on the 50:30:20 rule, you can now work out what, in an ideal world, you should be spending each month. This is your 50:30:20 budget.

DO THIS > WHAT IS YOUR IDEAL SPENDING

- Set aside 50 per cent of your income to pay for everyday 'needs' – This is your budget for all things essential.
- Set aside 30 per cent of your income to pay for 'wants' – This is your budget for all things non-essential but 'nice to have'.
- Set aside 20 per cent of your income for your long-term 'goals' – This is the bit your future self will thank you for. Remember the goals you made in Step 1 of the GFY Money Plan? Keep them in mind. Depending on which step of the plan you're on, this is where you put your goals budget: save for an emergency fund, pay off your debts, boost your emergency fund or invest.

Once you've calculated your own 50:30:20 budget you should have three figures: your needs budget, wants budget and goals budget. From here, you can work out both your annual budget and monthly budget.

WHAT IS YOUR IDEAL SPENDING?

	Monthly spending (£)	% of monthly post-tax income*
NEEDS		50%
WANTS		30%
GOALS		20%

*I've called it 'ideal' for a reason. If you have unavoidably high living costs, live in an expensive city or have a lower salary, then it's totally fine to adapt the 50:30:20. If a 20 per cent goals budget sounds steep, try starting with 10 per cent and tweak your wants and needs budgets accordingly. You can always work up. Equally, if you can set aside more than 20 per cent of your income for your goals, great! As with all things money: do what you can.

Step 4: Compare the two

Now you can compare your actual spending (Step 2) with your ideal spending (Step 3) and see where things need reining in. There might be a huge difference between the two and that's cool – nailing your budget is a long-term game and you might need to cut down your spending over time.

DO THIS > COMPARE ACTUAL AND IDEAL

Compare results from Step 2 and Step 3

- Go through your actual spending (Step 2) and look at where your spending can be tweaked (or drastically overhauled...) in order to meet your new 50:30:20 budget.

Questions to ask:

- Is that really a 'need'?
- Do I really want that 'want'?
- Could I get a better deal? / Is there a cheaper alternative?

DO THIS > THINK BIG PICTURE

Remember to also factor in the big wants that don't necessarily come every month. These are predictable and expensive outgoings, not unexpected emergencies (you've got your emergency fund for that). Take holidays as an example. Work out how much you can afford to spend on holidays each year in order to meet your wants budget, and then work backwards to calculate how much that would cost you each month up until the holiday. This way you can put aside some of your wants money each month and not need to worry when a big, predictable expense rolls around.

- Think of any big, predictable and infrequent purchases that might not have come up in the last three months, or any big purchases that you might have planned for the future. Don't confuse this with your 20 per cent goals budget! Ideally, these should come out of your wants and needs budget. Examples: Holidays, a new phone, your best friend's destination wedding, plastic surgery, hen-dos, insurance, Christmas presents.
- Calculate how much you plan to spend on these each year and then work backwards to figure out how much you would need to save each month, up until the date of purchase.

Step 5: Automate and track

Setting a budget is one thing, sticking to it is another. The best way to stay on track is to minimize the mental effort and stress involved in managing your cash flow.

Think of your finances as a well run business, with you the CEO: you don't just pocket the money that comes through the door. You think long term first: setting aside enough cash to pay employees, and reinvest in the business. It's only then then you pay yourself. The same goes for your finances. The moment any cash hits your account, think long term first; move your goals budget into its relevant place, before spending money on your wants and needs. Standing orders are your friend: set one up which transfers your goals budget, out of your current account every month. Where it goes will depend on where you are on the GFY Money Plan (see next step).

POST-TAX INCOME		
80% SPENDING MONEY		20% GOALS
MOVE % INTO SEPARATE ACCOUNT TO COVER PREDICTABLE MONTHLY EXPENSES	KEEP THE REST IN CURRENT ACCOUNT FOR DAY TO DAY SPENDING	MOVE TO GOAL ACCOUNT

Once you've transferred your goals budget, you've just got your wants and needs budget to worry about. You don't actually have to track these individually. The idea of separating wants and needs is to help build awareness around your spending and guidance on where you might want to cut things back. To keep things simple, you can simply combine the two to form an overall monthly spending budget which would make up 80 per cent of your post-tax income (30 per cent wants + 50 per cent needs). Once you've moved your 20 per cent goals budget out of your account, it can be helpful to then separate the 80 per cent that is left into predictable monthly expenses (utility bills, Netflix subscription, savings towards holidays) and your day to day expenses (eating out, groceries, travel), keeping each in a different account.

However, if you're a tracking fiend and the idea of sticking firmly to the 50 per cent and 30 per cent split sounds fun, get yourself a budgeting or banking app which is able to track your spending within each category.

DO THIS >

AUTOMATE YOUR CREDIT CARD PAYMENTS

For credit card users: if you use a credit card the same budgeting rules apply, but also set up a direct debit from your current account that automatically pays off your credit card bill every month.

Step 6: Goals

The best bit about the 50:30:20 method is that you'll quickly get closer to your goals whilst also having permission to spend money on the fun stuff. You've already set up a standing order which shifts your 20 per cent goals budget out of your current account every month. However, where it goes will depend on which step of the GFY Money Plan you're on*.

---

* For further information on budgeting and money saving go to gofundyourself.co

Use the following diagram to work out where your goals budget should go:

GFY Money Plan	Where to put your goals budget?
STEP 2 – Start an emergency fund	An easy access savings account
STEP 3 – Pay off expensive debts	Pay debts (see the GFY get out of debt plan on pp. 164–9)
STEP 5 – Boost your emergency fund	Savings account or cash equivalent (p. 196)
STEP 6 – Invest	Investment provider (you could continue to save in cash and invest a set % of your goals budget (p. 214–5)
STEP 7 – Live and give	Enjoy, keep investing and consider giving a portion away

Debt

The trouble is, access to credit plays into one of the greatest challenges that our human brains face: delayed gratification. Never have our minds been more challenged when having things is so accessible and the feeling of owning them so fun. It's not just the interest rates that we should be worried about, but the risk too. When it comes to buying in cash you become the true owner of whatever it is you're buying, which means you can also become the seller. So, if life goes pear-shaped and you really need the money, you're at liberty to sell – it's your stuff. On finance, however, not only do you have to worry about keeping repayments up, but you have nothing to sell either, putting you at risk of repossession and credit score damage.

You already know why buying in cash and avoiding debt tends to be the best way to spend money, but not all debt is created equal. Like first dates, debt can be good, but also really, really bad.

Good debt

Is a sensible investment in your financial future, leaves you better off in the long run and won't have a negative impact on your overall financial well-being. Usually this means debt with a low or no interest rate but be sure to look out for high charges or penalties. Good debt includes:

- **Student loan:** Because graduates tend to earn more than non-graduates, taking out a student loan can be a good investment. The interest rates are relatively low and you only have to repay the loan once you've reached an earnings threshold
- **Mortgage:** We all need somewhere to live and, unless you're extremely fortunate, the chances are you'll need to borrow money in order to buy a house. Houses not only put a roof over your head, they are also big financial assets, which are likely to grow in value over time
- **Investing in your own business:** Starting a business requires upfront investment, so taking out a loan to help you get your idea off the ground could pay dividends in

the long run. Of course this all depends on whether your business is a success, so make sure you are sensible and have a realistic plan of action (pp. 88–99)

- **Buying a car you can afford:** If paying in cash isn't an option and travelling by car is a necessity then buying a car on finance *could* be worth it. Make sure you're getting the best deal possible and that you can afford both the running costs and repayment
- **0 per cent interest** – CAN be good debt providing you're clued up on any sneaky fees. Whilst an interest free (0 per cent APR) deal can be a great way of spreading cost, rates often spike after a set period

Bad debt

Is debt that you are unlikely to be able to afford in the long run and, eventually, makes you financially worse off. It tends to be spending on things that lose their value quickly and do not generate long-term income. Bad debt includes:

- **Impulse purchases:** Sure, that two-week trans-Siberian odyssey seemed like a great idea at the time, but a month or two down the line, not so much. It's boring but calculating the long-term affordability of any kind of loan is vital. Nobody else will do it for you!
- **Very expensive debt:** Sometimes higher rates of interest might be worth it but some loans are just all round bad guys. I'm looking at you, payday and cash advance loans

GFY + HOW TO BE GOOD AT CREDIT

If buying in cash really isn't a viable option here are some tips to make sure you get the best deal possible:

- Put down the largest cash deposit you can – can you postpone the purchase for a month or two to rack up some savings?
- Compare deals, look at the total cost of borrowing, including interest and all charges over the term of the loan
- Negotiate discount for purchasing part of the item in cash
- Explore low-interest personal loans or 0 per cent credit cards, not just the most convenient financing option provided by the retailer
- Be realistic about what you can afford on a monthly basis. Will you still have enough to contribute to your goals budget and pay any running costs on top of that?
- Think about future credit needs: personal loans will be considered if applying for a mortgage and not keeping up with repayments can affect your credit rating

The GFY get out of debt plan

As a rule of thumb: if you can't afford it and don't need it, then don't buy it; but life is messy and bad debt happens. So how do you get out of it? The next section looks at the practicalities of organizing and getting out of debt you don't want.

1. Prioritize

First things first, you need to focus on your priority debts. These aren't always the most expensive debts but rather the ones with the biggest consequences for not paying them off. Use the following table to check if you've got any of the following and, if you do, pay them off as soon as possible.

PRIORITY DEBTS

Type of debt	Consequences of non-payment
Mortgage payments or secured loan	Repossession of your house
Rent	Eviction
Council tax	A visit from bailiffs, money taken from wages, money taken from benefits, debt secured against home, bankruptcy or imprisonment
Child maintenance	A visit from bailiffs, money taken from wages, money taken from benefits or imprisonment
Magistrates' court fines	A visit from bailiffs, money taken from wages, money taken from benefits or imprisonment
Tax, VAT or National Insurance	A visit from bailiffs, money taken from wages, bankruptcy, county court judgment (CCJ)
County court judgment	A visit from bailiffs, a charging order or money taken from wages
TV licence	A fine
Gas or electricity	Disconnection, money taken from benefits
Hire purchase or logbook loan	Repossession, county court judgment (CCJ)
Telephone	Disconnection, county court judgment (CCJ)

IN EMERGENCY, ASK FOR HELP!

If you're struggling to even pay off your priority debts each month, don't worry – there are things you can do:

- Talk to the lender immediately to see if you can lower your monthly payments
- Make sure you're getting the best possible deal on your utilities
- Speak to your local council to check you're in the correct council tax band

If you're facing a sudden debt emergency, such as court action, bailiffs or repossession, get free independent help immediately. A non-profit debt counsellor will be able to talk to the court, bailiff or creditor on your behalf. See pp. 175–7 for advice on money and your mental health. Check out gofundyourself.co for further resources.

2. Organize your non-priority debts

Once you've paid off your priority debts, you can address your non-priority debts.

Remember, non-priority doesn't mean they aren't important, it simply means the consequences of non-payment aren't quite as serious. That being said, non-payment can still involve being taken to court or bailiffs collecting money from you. Not to mention the hefty interest you can end up paying. Not fun.

Non-priority debts include:

- Overdrafts
- Personal loans
- Bank or building society loans
- Money borrowed from friends or family
- Credit card, store card debts or payday loans

Look over your debts and work out if you can reduce the interest you're paying. You can do this with a balance transfer which is when you get a new credit card that pays off the debts on your old cards. Either do this with a 0 per cent deal where there is no interest for a set period (but there will be a fee), or it may make sense to go for a card with a higher interest rate initially, but works out cheaper in the long run.

DO THIS > ORGANIZE YOUR NON-PRIORITY DEBTS

Use the table below to select the debts that apply to you, writing down the total amount you owe and the interest rate.

Type of debt	Interest rate	Amount owed

3. Choose a method

You should always keep up your minimum monthly payments to avoid falling behind but ideally you should look to pay off as much as you can afford each month (just make sure that there are no penalty charges for overpaying). If you're sticking to the 80:20 budget, then your 20 per cent goals budget should be directed at your debts. If you can't afford 20 per cent, that's OK, just do what you can.

However, if you have multiple non-priority debts, it can be tricky to know which ones to pay off first. Choosing one of the following strategies can help you to get debt-free faster whilst also minimizing the interest you pay.

Method 1 – Highest interest first

What? This approach means prioritizing debts with the highest interest rates.
How? Order your debts from highest to lowest interest rates and, starting with the most expensive, pay them off one by one (remembering to keep up with minimum payments of any others).
Why? Technically the most cost-effective strategy, this method minimizes the amount of interest you end up paying. For debts with very high interest rates, this method may be best.

Method 2 – Snowballing

What? This approach means prioritizing the debt with the smallest balance.

How? Order your debts from lowest to highest balance and pay them off one by one, starting with the smallest debt (remembering to keep up with minimum payments of any others).

Why? Whilst you may end up paying more in the long run, the thinking goes that by starting with the smallest debts, you quickly get a sense of achievement that motivates you to keep up with your debt repayments. If there isn't much difference in the interest rates of your debts, this method may be best.

Choosing a method is a personal thing. Once you've completed your debt table, think about which method you're most likely to be motivated by. This will depend on the kind of rates you're paying and the size of your debts.

GFY + HOW TO HELP YOURSELF

If you know that spending money and getting into debt might be something you struggle with, there are a few steps you can take to make spending just a little harder:

- Make it more difficult to spend money online. Delete your card details from your web browser
- Talk to friends and family about your triggers and warning signs so they can help you, and ask someone to hold you accountable for sticking to your debt plan
- Ask your bank to add a note to your credit file to make accessing debt harder
- Consider avoiding credit cards completely

Money and love

What's mine is mine and what's yours is mine.

Anon.

Love may know no bounds, but it still needs a utility bill paying and a romantic getaway budgeted for. The statistics are sobering: disputes over money are the second leading reason for divorce, close behind infidelity. When it comes to faithfulness in relationships, we're clear about setting boundaries pretty early on: chats about exclusivity and 'defining the relationship' are usually muttered within the first few months of dating. But what about money? When should we talk about it and, more to the point, how on earth do you manage it as a couple?

Of course, there are the financial practicalities that come with living together: how you'll split bills and pay for dinner, but the real challenge has very little to do with what you do with money and everything to do with your feelings about it. A new relationship is a collision of values and opinions, with money and love an emotional hotbed of contentious topics. We not only bring our own financial situation to the table but with it our trailing financial baggage: inherited values and beliefs around how money should and shouldn't be managed as a couple. Just as those values have an effect on our own financial decision making, they can trigger problems in our relationships too. If, according to you, money is power, you can only imagine what that might do to your self-worth when your partner earns more. This is why it's a good idea to get a hold on your own financial mindset (p. 148), before you bring them to the relationship table.

A friend recently opened up about how she and her boyfriend manage their money; he noted how their childhood experiences had drastically shaped their opinions and attitude towards it. 'My parents went through a horrible and expensive divorce which has definitely left me quite defensive and protective when it comes to money. She on the other hand feels very strongly that money should be shared completely.' As with most challenges in a relationship, opening up and communicating is key but, at the end of the day, something will have to give. The chances are you won't be on quite the same page, so use money as an opportunity to bring the two of you together: create a set of shared values that you can both get on board with. You're a team and money is your tool to create a shared life together.

GFY + LOVE AND MONEY METHODS

As part of your conversation on money, discussions around the practicalities of how to manage it are bound to emerge. There is no one-size-fits-all approach but, generally, there are four options to choose from:

- **The Separates** – Keep everything separate and create your own rules for paying joint expenses. This could be by splitting them 50/50 or by proportion of how much you earn relative to the other person.

- **The Sharers** – Pool your resources and have a shared account from which all your outgoings are paid. Make sure you're both on the same page when it comes to what determines a financial want vs a need.

- **The Hybrid** – Rather than go all in, create a shared account into which you both contribute a sum each month. This is then used to pay for shared expenses such as utility bills, shared dinners together and rent. You decide what's shared and what's not.

- **The Allowance** – If one partner isn't earning or is earning less than the other, the main earner could transfer a specified amount into their partner's account. What the allowance covers is up to you but it's important that both parties are happy with the arrangement and that the money isn't viewed as a 'favour' from one to the other.

If you decide on some sort of shared arrangement, you don't need to go all in, overnight. Try opening a shared account and contribute a small amount each month. If all goes well and you're both happy with how things are working out, you can begin to increase your contributions from there.

Relationships and debt

Remember, being married to or living with someone who has a bad credit score won't affect your own. However, if you take out a loan together, or open a shared account, it might. So before combining your finances, check your credit scores to understand whether there's an option that benefits you both.

The legalities of love

Living together

Couples who live together but who aren't married (sometimes referred to as cohabiting couples) have no legal status under UK law. This means that were you to split up there's no saying as to who is entitled to what. Cohabitation agreements and declarations of trust (in the case of buying property) are legal agreements that outline the rights and obligations of each partner towards the other. For example, if you buy a property together and contribute different deposits, or if one of you stops working to look after kids, what would those imbalances mean if the worst were to happen? Who would be entitled to what? Whilst declarations of trust that outline the details of property ownership are legally binding, meaning they will be upheld in a court of law, cohabitation agreements are not. However, providing a cohabitation agreement has been properly drafted, and both parties have sought independent legal advice, then it's very likely to be followed by the court.

Marriage / civil partnership

The ultimate commitment. Romantically? Yes. Financially? Even more so. If you're married, in a civil partnership or just thinking about tying the knot, get familiar with the following benefits:

- **Marriage Allowance** – If a husband or wife isn't earning (or is earning less than the personal income tax allowance), then they can transfer 10 per cent of their personal allowance to the other partner, providing they are basic rate taxpayers. At the time of writing, this would mean the higher earner would not pay 20 per cent tax on an additional £1,190, making them £238 better off. If the marriage allowance applies to you, you'll need to complete a very short application form on the HMRC website

- **Inheritance Tax** – As a couple, not only can you leave everything to your husband or wife tax-free, you can transfer any unused inheritance tax allowance to your partner, effectively doubling your allowance
- **Capital Gains Tax** – CGT is a tax you pay on the profit you make when you sell assets such as share investments or a second property; however, you can give anything to your partner tax-free
- **Pension** – Most private pension schemes allow you to pass on a percentage of your pension to your spouse or civil partner when you die. Be sure to check the rules!
- **Wills** – Even if you haven't made a will, your spouse or civil partner automatically inherits some of the money and/or property that you leave

Unlike cohabiting couples, spouses and civil partners have certain rights under UK law. In the case of divorce, this means it's likely that the matrimonial assets (financial assets that you and/ or your spouse acquire during the course of your marriage) will be divided up between you. They might be split 50/50 but this isn't always the case as commonly believed.

Money and the mind

Jerome was only twenty. He'd just secured his first job as a courier, delivering blood to hospitals in and around London on his beloved motorbike. He'd told friends how he'd be able to make upwards of £1,500 a month, a wage that would afford a holiday with his girlfriend.

It started with two £65 traffic fines. Fines that on their own he might have been able to shoulder. But when his motorbike broke down, an expense that his zero-hour contract said was his responsibility, Jerome was stuck. Within months, the £130 had multiplied into a monstrous debt of over £1,000 and before long he was pursued by bailiffs. Too ashamed to confide in his family, Jerome's internet history revealed manic searches between payday loans and information on suicide. It was when a bailiff seized his motorbike, a necessity for his work and the only ability he had to pay off the debt, that Jerome sent a loving text to his girlfriend, and walked out of his family home for the last time. His older brother discovered his body a day later.

Money, debt and mental health are inextricably linked. In the UK, the statistics speak for themselves:

- One in four adults will have a mental health problem at some point in their life
- One in two adults with debts has a mental health problem
- One in four people with a mental health problem is also in debt

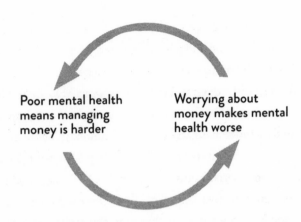

Poor mental health means managing money is harder

Worrying about money makes mental health worse

Nobody is too rich or too poor to suffer from mental health problems and there is a near infinite source of financial stress that can affect anyone. We have the fundamentals to worry about: being unable to house, clothe and feed ourselves. And then there is a whole load of more complex financial challenges: redundancy, debt, addiction, health concerns, economic pressure, separation, children. All these factors feed into a vicious cycle: money worries affect our mental health and poor mental health makes managing money even harder.

If it's your spending that's either causing or caused by a mental health problem, mental health charity Mind recommends that you first try to understand your behaviour.

- Think about when you spend money and why
- Think about what aspects of money make your mental health worse – is it talking to people, opening envelopes, confrontation or when you slip up? Or is it something else?

- It could help to keep a diary of your spending. Try to record what you spend and why. Keep a record of your mood too. This could help you work out any triggers or patterns
- When you understand more about your behaviour you can think about what might help. Sometimes just being aware of these patterns can help you feel more in control

Money worries should never mean the end. It may take some time, but there is always a solution and there are plenty of places and people who want to and can help you. This could mean practical assistance such as setting up an affordable repayment plan or emotional support and seeking therapy. Your GP or another health professional may be able to provide a Debt and Mental Health Evidence Form. This can help make sure that creditors take your mental health problems into account. For more information on managing debt and getting mental health support, go to mind.org.uk.

PART V

INVEST IT

PART 1: SAVE AND INVEST

What is investing?
Tackling generational beliefs
Are you ready?
What am I actually investing in?
Funds
Where should I invest?
Ethical investing
What next?

PART 2: GETTING ON THE PROPERTY LADDER

A letter to aspiring homeowners
Can I buy?
Why are you doing this?
The GFY guide to getting on the property ladder
Live and give

PART 1: SAVE AND INVEST

In 'Spend it' we looked at budgeting and how to set aside 20 per cent of your income for your long-term goals, but if you're thinking about stock-piling your cash like some kind of drug lord…no, no, no. In this chapter we'll be looking at how you can put your money to work through investing (Step 6 of the GFY Money Plan), helping you to reach your goals faster.

In Part 1 we'll look at why sitting on cash is actually losing you money, how to leave a multi-million-pound fortune and why you don't need the wisdom of Warren Buffett to make money on the stock market. If you listed 'buying a property' as one of your money goals in Step 1 of the GFY Money Plan, Part 2 is for you. Covering the essentials of home-ownership, it'll help you work out if buying a property is *actually* what you want whilst talking you through the steps from renter to homeowner.

Let me tell you the story of two investors.

Grace Groner was born in 1909, in a small farming community in Lake County, Illinois. She was orphaned at the age of twelve and, thanks to a generous family in her town, was given the chance to attend Illinois' liberal arts school, Lake Forest

College. To all who knew Grace she was a kind and humble lady who led a relatively normal life. She never married or had children and for most of her days lived in a small one-bedroom apartment above a cinema. This made her secret all the more confusing. Following her death, her will revealed that she'd left a staggering $7 million to her old college. Everyone who knew Grace wondered how she had acquired such enormous wealth. Where had the money come from?

Grace hadn't won the lottery, nor was she the lucky recipient of a trust fund. Her wealth could be explained by a simple decision she had made at the age of twenty-six. A decision just as ordinary as her life but one with spectacular consequences. Whilst working as a secretary for Abbott Laboratories, Grace purchased three $60 shares in the company. Shares which, over the course of her working life, had split multiple times, and paid dividends (a share of a company's profits, paid to its shareholders), which she'd reinvested every year. She kept her accumulated wealth a complete secret and before her death set up a foundation that would continue to support college students at her alma mater for years to come.

Only a few weeks after Grace's death, the story of another investor made the headlines. Richard Fuscone had filed for personal bankruptcy. Harvard educated, Richard had forged a glittering career in banking, culminating in the position of vice chairman at Merrill Lynch in Latin America. Richard's success meant he could retire at the early age of forty-nine and, after witnessing the retirement of old friends, he believed his best years were ahead of him. With his newfound freedom, he committed his time to charitable activities in the local community, whilst also using his already significant wealth to start his own investment firm. Of course, with his retirement came a lavish lifestyle. He purchased the property of his dreams, one of the largest in the area, and borrowed $12 million to fund its extension. He was the envy of all his friends, who would enjoy extravagant parties atop his glass-covered swimming pool. However, it was during the financial crisis of 2008 that things took an ugly turn. The investment firm that he had founded, and sunk $25 million of his own money into, failed. With debts of over $13 million, Richard's extravagant and flamboyant lifestyle was at an end. Not only had his business collapsed but, with it, his ability to maintain his $66,000 a month mortgage and payments on the vast debts he had accumulated. After selling his home for a significant loss, Richard emerged from bankruptcy and began to rebuild his wealth from scratch.

These stories aren't meant to fuel the stereotypes of 'bad bankers' and dodgy credit. Nor are they to say that the only way to wealth is to live frugally and stockpile shares in the company you work for. There is no doubt that Grace's fortune can be credited somewhat to luck, just as Richard's can be put down to misfortune. As with all investments, timing, circumstance and opportunity are key.

However, the stories of Grace and Richard hold a valuable lesson, not in what makes a good investment, but in what a good investor looks like. They show us that success with money isn't about what you know or who you are. Nor is it exclusive to those who work in banking or have received a prestigious education. Investing is much more about behaviour. It's about understanding that building wealth is a slow game and having the patience to get yourself there.

It's easy to see why we might think otherwise. Billion-dollar industries have been built on telling people what they should invest in and which stock will make them a fortune, rather than helping them look at the bigger, and arguably more important, picture: the behaviours that make an investor successful. As a result, our perception of investing has been warped. 'Investor' conjures up Wolf-of-Wall-Street-esque images that we don't identify with: shouty men in pinstripe suits, trading pits and wodges of banknotes. When, in reality, it's something wholly different. Investing, particularly investing well, isn't about who you are, it's largely about the small behaviours and choices that you make on a day to day basis. We've been fed the idea that patience is for the boring. Want to buy a car that is twice your annual salary? No problem, here's a monthly payment plan. Need your kitchen renovating but only have £300 to your name? Just pop it on our store credit card. Whilst Richard's ambition was on a completely different scale, his attitude was just the same. He wanted it all and he wanted it now.

The key to Grace's financial success wasn't that she had some miraculous gift for spotting undervalued shares. In fact, the way she made her fortune could have been replicated by investing in a number of other companies at the time. Her gift was patience, which enabled her to take advantage of the greatest investing trick of all: compounding.

Investing principle 1: Compounding

Compound interest is the eighth wonder of the world. He who understands it, earns it… he who doesn't… pays it.

Albert Einstein

I explained earlier how Grace didn't take any profits and instead reinvested her dividend payments every year. This meant that instead of cashing out and spending any gains she had made, she left her investments to it. Over the years, Grace wasn't just making money on her original investment, but also on the reinvested profit from the previous years. As an example, let's say that as a twenty-two-year old, you made a £1,000 investment that was expected to provide you with a 10 per cent return every year. After year one you'd still have your original £1,000 plus a £100 gain, leaving you with a total of £1,100. In year two you'd earn another 10 per cent on your original £1000, as well as 10 per cent on the gain you made in year one, which would be another £10. So now you have a total of £1,210. By year three, you'd be making returns on the gains from year one and year two… and so on. It's this cumulative effect that's called compounding and, over time, its effects can be life changing.

Let's say you continue with your investment plan: but after investing the initial £1,000 you also contribute an additional £10 a month to the investment, which returns on average 10 per cent a year. After forty years, you'd have a staggering £100,000! Even when you adjust for inflation you're looking at close to £50,000. It's no wonder that Einstein described compounding as the eighth wonder of the world.

THE POWER OF COMPOUNDING

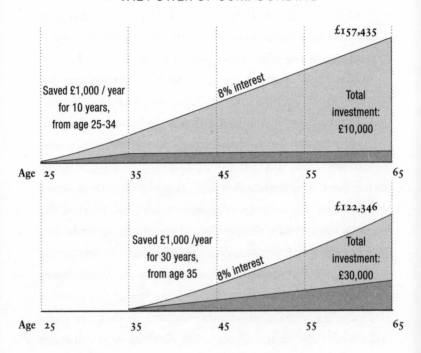

What is investing?

Before we go any further, let's clarify what we mean by 'investing'.

Investing: the purchase of assets or goods with the aim of making more wealth in the future. Usually, this means buying something that will either provide you with income as a result of holding onto it, such as a house that you buy and rent out or an income stock. It can also mean buying something that will increase in value whilst holding it, so that you can sell it for a profit later down the line. This profit is called capital gain. This might be a house you buy to live in, or a growth stock. (Income stock and growth stock are defined on p. 195.)

So investing can mean a whole load of different things but the defining factor is that the buyer of an investment believes that at some point in the future, it will increase their wealth. Portfolio income describes any kind of income you receive from investments. Investors hope that they'll make a higher return than in a traditional bank account offering a steady interest rate of say, 0.5 per cent. However, with this potential for higher reward comes higher risk and uncertainty. Whilst that level of risk differs across assets, investors have to accept that their investments, whatever they might be, could depreciate in value and end up losing them money.

Of course, plenty of people do want the security of a bank and there's nothing wrong with that. They want stability, not big returns. In fact, it actually makes sense to keep some cash locked away. As we've seen, financial crises tend to arrive like claps of thunder out of a clear blue sky, so protecting your money is critical. However, investing doesn't have to be all or nothing. There is a spectrum of investment options depending on your confidence, appetite for risk and long-term goals.

You can also invest in other assets such as property, which we'll look at in Part 2. However, what we most commonly mean by investing, and what we're referring to in Part 1, is buying assets from a market. Not the fruit and veg kind, but a marketplace selling financial goods. The stock market being the main one.

Tackling generational beliefs

You can never plan the future by the past.

Edmund Burke

The opinions and habits we are exposed to during our early life are hard to shake. Whilst our own experiences and those of people around us make up a minute fraction of what's actually happening in the world, they shape the majority of our beliefs around how we think the world works. This is particularly true when it comes to our attitudes to personal finance. For most of us, we get our first glimpse into the workings of money from our parents, which explains why, very often, our own attitudes towards it are shaped by their own financial successes or failures. Upbringings and childhoods vary wildly but there are a handful of inherited beliefs and fears that are consistent across different generations.

For my generation, growing up throughout the nineties and noughties, it's likely that we've watched the value of our parents' properties flourish and undoubtedly had to sit through sickening tales of just how little they bought their first house for and how much it's worth now. Particularly in the UK where the dream of home ownership runs to the very core of our being, we tend to believe that the best and most desirable investment of all is a house. When it comes to the stock market, however, we freak out. Most of us will have already witnessed at least one financial crisis. Be it the dot-com bubble of 2000 or the credit crisis of 2008, we've seen the stock market at its ugliest. The 2008 crisis in particular left the reputation of the financial sector in tatters, and with it our confidence in the markets; perhaps you've witnessed the direct effects of these global crises on the lives of those closest to you. Compounded by the fact that we're just not taught anything in school about the inner workings of the economy or financial sector, it's no wonder that younger generations are gun shy when it comes to investing. We've seen or heard about the damage it can do and think we've learned valuable lessons from it: seeking comfort in cash, avoiding stocks and shares and developing an obsession with home ownership. However, whilst the last twenty years have proved that the stock market can be damn scary at times, they haven't disproved its potential to make you money in the long run.

Investing principle 2: Time

Imagine you've just bought a puppy (let's call her Lola) and you're taking her on a walk through the park. You have a plan; it's a nice day and you're going to grab a coffee when you reach the other side. Lola, however, is on a mission of her own. She's flitting from left to right, jumping up at passers-by. There's no controlling her. But, in the long run, you know where she'll end up. The same goes for investing: Lola the puppy refers to the short-term unpredictable movement of the stock market. Yet, historically, in the long run, things have always headed in a positive direction for sensible investors.

For example, let's say you picked any day between January 1970 and July 2017 and decided to invest for that day only. Based on the historical stock market data, you'd have a 53.5 per cent chance of making money — in other words, on only 53.5 per cent of those days did the stock market increase in value, just a little bit better than putting your money on black at the casino. Now let's say you invested for any one year during the same period. This time your chance of making money will have gone up to 77.8 per cent. Invest for ten years and your chances go up to 98.6 per cent. In fact, nobody who invested in the stock market for more than 11.1 years during this period would have lost any money!

Looking over the past ninety years, the average annual total return for the S&P 500 Index (a collection of 500 US stocks intended to reflect the overall return of the stock market as a whole) was 9.8 per cent, an encouraging figure when you consider the interest rate on your savings account. However, statistics like this can be very misleading; unlike your savings account which promises you 1 per cent per cent each year, an investor in the S&P 500 Index can't expect a certain 10 per cent annual growth and to see their investments double every ten years. Firstly, once you adjust for inflation, this figure falls to around 7 per cent but you also need to consider that, whilst the average return might be 10 per cent, it's rare that the stock market is ever close to that average in any given year – it often falls vastly over or vastly under that figure. In other words, it's unpredictable.

Take a look at this table showing the average annual returns of S&P 500 over the past twenty years:

S&P 500 INDEX (1930–2019)

S&P 500 Annual Returns *							
1999	19.53%	2004	8.99%	2009	23.45%	2014	11.39%
2000	-10.14%	2005	3.00%	2010	12.78%	2015	-0.73%
2001	-13.04%	2006	13.62%	2011	0.00%	2016	9.54%
2002	-23.37%	2007	3.53%	2012	13.41%	2017	19.42%
2003	26.38%	2008	-38.49%	2013	29.60%	2018	-6.24%

* The annual gain or loss in the S&P 500 stock index from 1999 to 2018. Dividends not included.

You'll see that, whilst over the past twenty years it has increased in value more than it decreased, the performance varies wildly year on year. This is why investing for short amounts of time is really risky – you could win big, but you could also lose big.

It's also why it's a bad idea to try to 'time the market', i.e. predicting when it's a good time to invest. Even professional traders with all the tools and algorithms have very limited success when it comes to strategically dipping in and out of the market in an attempt to avoid the drops.

So now, let's plot the performance of the S&P 500 over eighty years (see next page). You can still see the annual rises and falls that are shown in the table but over the long term the value goes up.

You see that what happens in the short term isn't an accurate predictor of long-term performance. A much more successful approach is to invest for the long term, which, in investing speak, is five years plus.

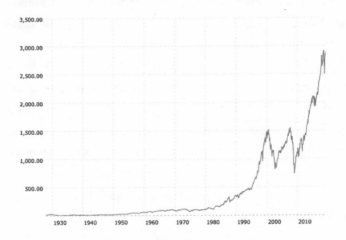

The point is, ups and downs are inevitable, but it's over the long term that these bumps are ridden out. The longer you're in the market, the less likely you are to lose money. In fact, the odds say, you'll make it.

If you take anything away from this chapter, it should be that investing can be a universally powerful tool but even more so for our generation. Working harder, living longer, smaller pensions, lower wages, expensive social care. I won't bore you with 101 other depressingly predictable reasons that thinking about and preparing for the future is important. You know it's a good idea but sensible rarely serves as a call to action.

Let's think about investing differently: not as a way to do our unretired, still-renting octogenarian selves a small favour, but instead as a brilliant opportunity to make a dent in the unwavering intergenerational wealth gap.

We have a competitive advantage when it comes to investing. We hold more of the most precious resource on earth: time.

Not only do we have more time to capitalize on the phenomenon of compounding, but we have time to ride out those bumps in the market. In fact, for us, bumps are a great thing.

The goal of investing is simple: buy low; sell high. Or buy a little bit regularly (as is the case with the drip feed strategy see p. 214). So, whilst drops in the market mean our investments might be worth less for a while, it gives us an opportunity to invest more at a lower price. Retirement isn't coming soon, so when older generations are cashing out, we can cash in.

Are you ready?

All things being equal, the sooner you start investing the better, but there are a few things to tick off before you get started. You might have the money to invest but it's important to think about whether it could first be put to better use, or whether you have the money at all. Let's recap on the GFY Money Plan (see p. 9–15) and the five steps to take before you invest.

Step 1: You've got goals

Step 2: You've got an emergency fund

Step 3: You've paid off expensive debts

Step 4: You have a pension and have maximized contributions

Step 5: You've boosted your emergency fund

Step 6: Invest!

In theory, you are now at liberty to throw your money at the markets with the exuberance of Jordan Belfort, but before you do – please read on!

What am I actually investing in?

You've made some money moves and you're ready to get going, but first we need to cover the essentials. Let me be straight with you: we're straying into pretty unsexy territory right now. I'd probably file this under the 'I'm on an awkward first date and need something to talk about other than the logistics of my daily commute' category of conversation. But stay with me, this is important.

To get started, let's look at the kind of assets you're actually buying when you 'invest'.

For simplicity, we can break investment assets down into three categories: Shares, Bonds and Cash, each of which offer a different level of risk.

Asset		Risk level
Shares (sometimes called stocks or equities)	• If a company were a cake, think of shares as one tiny slice. Owning a slice is often referred to as having 'equity' in that company. • Whilst some companies are privately owned, others are public, which means that they sell their shares on the stock market (also known as being 'listed') as a way to raise money, or 'capital'. Investors can buy and sell the shares.	⋆⋆⋆

Asset		Risk level
	However, shares carry risk, some more than others; unexpected events and negative developments affect the value of the company, the dividends it pays, and therefore the price of its shares. If the company goes bust, your shares do too and you can lose all your money. There are three types of shares that you can make money from. 'Stock' is the generic term used to describe ownership of part of a company: 1. **Growth stocks:** Companies that are expected to increase in value and therefore can be sold for a higher amount at a later date. If the company does well, and goes up in value, the price of your share goes up too. This is called capital appreciation. 2. **Income stocks:** Companies that reward shareholders with a proportion of the profit. This reward is called a dividend (paid quarterly). These tend to be large, well-established companies that grow at a slow rate but make large profits. An income stock can also be a value stock. 3. **Value stocks:** These are companies usually trading at a price below where it appears it should be. For example, if a fast food chain became embroiled in a PR scandal which found that their veggie burgers weren't really veggie, their share price would probably drop. An investor might see this as an opportunity to buy undervalued shares in a company on the belief that memories are short and it would soon recover.	

Asset		Risk level
Bonds / Fixed income	• In short, bonds are like IOUs issued by governments or companies wanting to raise money, also known as capital. • You lend them money and, in exchange, you receive a fixed rate of interest (or 'coupon') over a set period of time. This is why they are sometimes called 'fixed income' investments. • Once the time period is up (known as reaching 'maturity'), you get back your original investment. • For example, you might invest £5,000 in a five-year bond paying an interest rate of 3 per cent per year. Assuming you hold the bond to maturity, you will receive £1,500 in interest over the six years. • In terms of investment risk, bonds sit somewhere between shares and cash. The least risky are government and big corporates bonds, but even these have been known to go bust. However, they are less risky than shares given that failing companies have a duty to pay back bondholders before shareholders. • Different types of bonds carry different levels of risk with 'Investment grade bonds' ranging from AAA to BBB according to Standard and Poor's rating agency. • The UK government issues bonds; they're sometimes called gilts or gilt-edged securities.	**
Cash or cash equivalents	• In terms of security, cash is the safest store of wealth (providing you aren't literally stuffing it under your bed), however, with interest rates so low the returns on locking your savings away tend to be uninspiring. • Emergency funds need to be accessible, beware the Silent Savings Assassin: Inflation. As the cost of goods rise, the spending power of your cash diminishes, so make sure you have a savings account which is as close to the rate of inflation as possible. • Certain types of bonds can be classified as 'cash equivalents' because they carry virtually no risk. This includes some government and even corporate bonds.	*

Investing principle 3: Diversification

When it comes to choosing which assets to invest in, it's not a question of picking a stock or a bond that you like the look of and hoping for the best. Just as living off a diet of chocolate buttons and meat feast pizzas isn't likely to yield great results, the same goes for investing in a single asset. Investors diversify, holding a range of assets from different classes in order to meet their appetite for risk and goals. Drake himself is no stranger to the idea. In his song *Over My Dead Body*, he uses the popular phrase 'you win some and lose some' to explain that as long as your investments pay out overall, you're golden.

The idea is that by having a portfolio of investments, i.e. spreading your cash across a number of ventures, you reduce your exposure to any potential losses. Drake is saying that, sure, some investments might not work out but when you own just a little bit of lots of different companies, if one goes bust, this will have a much smaller impact on your entire portfolio than if you only had shares in one company alone.

Diversification operates at two levels, firstly holding multiple asset classes (stocks, bonds and cash) and also holding multiple investments within each of these classes.

Asset allocation is the proportion of stocks to bonds to cash that your portfolio contains and plays an important role in determining your risk.

GFY + A WORD ON... ASSET ALLOCATION

There is no 'perfect' balance when it comes to asset allocation, it's a personal thing and is dependent on factors such as your personal goals, your age and appetite for risk. However, the closer you get to retirement, or the closer you get to needing access to your money, then less risky investments make sense.

Short-term investors (< five years)

As we talked about in the GFY Money Plan (see pp. 9–15), if you're looking to use your money within the next five years, it's risky to invest in shares or a fund with a high proportion of shares. However, this doesn't mean you need to keep all your money in cash. Instead you could consider cash equivalents such as low-risk government bonds (see p. 196).

Long-term investors (> five years)

If you're in it for the long game and are happy to stash your cash for five or more years, then you can afford to take on some risk and build a portfolio with a mixture of shares, bonds and cash. The exact proportion will depend on how much risk you're comfortable with, which we'll get onto pp. 207–13.

Investing for retirement

If you're self-employed and opening a personal pension or you're just looking to tuck away a bit extra for your older years then the following equation is a useful rule of thumb for the proportion of shares you might hold:

110 – age = the percentage of shares held in your portfolio

The above number gives you the proportion of shares, and so the remainder should be held in bonds. Remember, the cash savings in your emergency fund are not part of your portfolio. Let's say you're twenty-seven. According to the equation, your retirement portfolio should contain roughly 83 per cent shares and 17 per cent bonds. It's also worth noting that the types of shares you want to hold might change as you get older; for example, as retirement approaches, investors reduce risk by adjusting their portfolio in favour of income shares over growth shares.

However, age aside, you should also think about your own personal tolerance for risk, which we'll look at shortly.

However, the easiest way to have a diverse investment portfolio is by investing in funds.

Funds

Now, unless you fancy yourself as a bit of a Gordon Gecko, most of us have neither the time nor inclination to be single-handedly selecting dozens of shares and bonds or anxiously checking the markets on our lunch breaks. Instead, there is a much easier way to have a 'diversified' portfolio: meet The Fund.

Say you're at work and you want a salad for lunch and this week you've totally failed at bringing in your own. I'd imagine what you'd do is pop down to the nearest shop or cafe and pick one up, ready made. Someone else has gone to the effort of buying all the ingredients, chopping them up and selling it to you for a price. The salad you're buying is like a share in a fund. You get the benefit of variety (which means diversification) without the faff of buying an entire week's worth of groceries.

Unlike buying a single bond or share, funds allow you to pool your money with other investors and buy into a broad range of shares, bonds or both, in one transaction, as opposed to buying them individually. If the value of the investments in the fund goes up, your share of the fund also increases in value, and vice versa of course. Funds are professionally managed which means that, rather than you deciding exactly which shares or bonds to invest in, a fund manager does it for you.

Funds have three major benefits:

- **Less risky** – Diversification means your money is spread across a wide range of assets
- **Usually cheaper** – You'll only be paying one lot of fees for every 'unit' of a fund you buy, as opposed to numerous sets of fees you would pay if you bought shares and bonds individually. We'll talk more about fees on p. 213
- **More investment opportunity** – Because you're pooling your money with other investors you have access to many more investments than if you were buying alone

To extend the salad analogy… there are plenty of different funds to choose from, each containing different things. Some funds might only be invested in bonds, others shares, and some a mixture of the two, which are called balanced funds. Some investors might choose to simply invest in a balanced fund as this takes care of asset allocation, whilst others might take a more bespoke approach and invest in a couple of different funds.

Funds also have specific themes, which determine their risk level. For example, UK government bonds are a much safer investment than a fund invested in emerging markets.

Examples of themes are as follows:

- **Geographic** – E.g. Shares in European or international companies or shares in emerging markets
- **Industry sector and thematic** – E.g. Shares in renewable energy, luxury goods, tech and healthcare companies
- **Investment types** – E.g. Solely corporate bonds or government bonds
- **Size of company** – E.g. Shares in FTSE 100 companies, or shares in small cap companies
- **Type of return** – E.g. Income stocks or growth stocks

DON'T PANIC! If this all seems super complicated, sit tight. Of course getting to grips with the fundamentals of how funds work is a good thing, but there is a way of investing that doesn't involve selecting your own funds or worrying about asset allocation. We'll get to this on p. 210–12.

GFY + A WORD ON... FUND FACTSHEETS

In terms of their thrill factor, they might not compete with the latest Netflix release, but fund factsheets are a useful source of information when it comes to getting your head around a fund, particularly if you opt for the DIY investing approach.

The fund factsheet will include information such as:

1. **The name of the fund:** e.g. Equity Growth Fund.
2. **The name of the company that's managing the fund:** e.g. ABC Investments.
3. **The objectives of the fund**: this will tell you whether the fund is designed to produce an income (income stocks) or to increase its value (growth stocks). It will also tell you in very broad terms what it is going to invest in (e.g. shares, bonds etc.) and whether it invests in companies in a certain location and/or of a certain size.
4. **Who the fund manager is**: these are the people who are responsible for deciding how money in that fund is invested. It may also tell you when the fund manager took over the management of that fund, useful to know especially if the relative performance of the fund has altered over time and since the change in fund manager.
5. **Fund or unit price**: this is the price of a unit in the fund.
6. **Asset allocation**: there may be a pie chart or a table showing what the fund is invested in, e.g. shares, property, bonds etc. It may give more detail than this, such as sectors, i.e. financials, healthcare, mining, retail etc.

7. **Top 10 holdings**: this is a list of the companies that the fund currently has the most money invested in. It will also tell you the percentage of the fund invested in each of those companies.

8. **Charges**: the fund factsheet gives you information about the charges you will pay to invest in the fund such as the initial charge, annual management charges payable to the fund manager, and ongoing administration charges.

9. **Performance**: the factsheet will normally have information on performance over the last year, three years and five years (or less, if it's a newer fund). It will also include how the sector has performed as a whole. The idea is that you can see whether the fund has done better or worse than average compared to similar funds.

10. **Minimal initial investment**: this tells you how much you can invest in the fund as a one-off initial investment and on an ongoing basis.

Types of fund

ETFs vs mutual funds

Funds vary not only in the kinds of investments they contain but also in how they are managed, where you buy and sell them, and how they are priced. The two types of fund worth knowing about are: exchange-traded funds (ETFs) and mutual funds.

The main difference is that ETFs are traded on an exchange (it's in the name!) just like a stock, so the price is constantly changing depending on supply and demand. However, a mutual fund (a 'unit trust' and 'open-ended investment companies' in the UK) can only be bought at one point in the trading day for a set price (called the net asset value). This is based on the current value of all the investments the fund contains. The price of an ETF is usually close to the net asset value but it can vary due to changes in supply and demand.

ETFs	MUTUAL FUNDS
Trades during trading day	Trades at a single point in the day (some less frequently)
Low operating expenses	Operating expenses vary
No investment minimums	Most have investment minimums

As with all funds, ETFs are professionally managed funds that pool your money with other investors. But the thing that sets ETFs apart from other funds is that you buy shares in ETFs from a stock exchange, just like shares in a company. This makes them super accessible, transparent and low cost.

Importantly, ETFs tend to be passive, meaning that they 'track' a market under a specific theme. For example, this might be an Index such as the FTSE 100, often called the Footsie (the 100 largest listed companies in the UK), or the performance of a specific asset such as government bonds. To do this, the fund manager is responsible for buying the relevant assets. For example, if the fund aims to track the performance of the FTSE

100, the fund manager simply buys shares, on behalf of all the investors, in all the FTSE 100 companies.

ETFs

ETFs are the vanilla ice cream of the investing world. They're no frills and widely available, and many investors sing the praises of the humble ETF, arguing that, in the long term, they outperform actively managed funds. In fact, in 2007, Warren Buffett (did someone say investor crush...?) won a $1 million bet after demonstrating that a hedge fund (the swankiest and arguably most complex kind of fund) couldn't outperform an S&P 500 index fund.

One of the big reasons that many investors are such fans of the ETF is how cheap they are relative to other funds. Because ETFs simply track a market, they're much simpler for a fund manager to maintain. For an active fund, on the other hand, it's a fund manager's duty to keep an eye on investments, communicate with Finance Directors, understand what's going on in the sector, and tweak the positions they hold in shares accordingly. This involves a lot of research, time and expertise, which means the fund is likely to charge higher fees than an ETF.

Active funds vs passive funds

Funds also vary in how they are managed. As a rule of thumb, ETFs tend to be passive funds given that they are usually set up to simply track an index or market. Mutual funds on the other hand can be either active or passive. If a fund is actively managed, this means that the fund has its very own human being (a.k.a. a fund manager) whose job is to continually assess the fund's investments. The goal is to 'beat the market', which means delivering higher growth than if, say, you'd invested in all the companies in the FTSE 100. Alternatively, a passive fund simply tracks the performance of a market segment or index. They're founded on the belief that trying to outsmart the market is a hit and miss affair and that, really, no one has an advantage when it comes to price or information.

Imagine two cars on a motorway, both headed in the same direction. A petrol-head in a souped-up sports car, nipping in and out of the traffic and aiming to beat every other vehicle on the road. This guy represents the active fund. The other, a family of four in a sturdy hatchback set on cruise control: the passive fund. The hatchback isn't in a hurry; they're sticking to the speed limit and keeping pace with the rest of the traffic. They're not breaking any records, just planning to get home in time for tea. Alternatively, the sports car provides all the glorious adrenaline highs you'd expect, albeit with the higher risk of nerve-wracking lows. It (hopefully) contains a highly skilled driver with unwavering confidence and excellent insight into what lies ahead. The same applies to a fund manager wanting to win the race of investment returns. Based on extensive research, the fund manager will invest in assets that they believe have the potential to perform well and, conversely, avoid assets that they think won't.

Investing principle 4: Risk and return

The stock market is a device for transferring money from the impatient to the patient.

Warren Buffett, CEO of Berkshire Hathaway

Nobody knows what the future holds. If we knew which of today's startups would be following in the footsteps of Google or Apple, we'd be sipping ice cold G&Ts on our own private islands in no time. It's this uncertainty that underpins all financial markets. Investing is simply speculation around the likelihood of an investment paying off. The reason we know that bonds are less risky than shares is that, historically, we know that shares are more likely to lose investors money than bonds. However, we also know that shares, particularly growth shares (stocks), have the potential to make investors a lot more money than bonds. It's this trade-off between risk and reward that investors are constantly at odds with. How much money are you willing to risk for the potential return?

Understanding your own risk profile is critical to good investing. Firstly, so that you won't pull the plug on your investments during the inevitable blips, but also so you can invest in the right kind of fund(s) and get your asset allocation on point.

Only you can know how much risk you're willing to take; however, these two principles might help you decide:

- **Time** – As Grace's story showed, time is the most powerful resource when it comes to investing. So, if you're in your twenties or thirties, you've got a huge advantage. That being said, it's a good idea to think about your time horizon. If you're investing for the long term, you can afford to take more risks as you've got more time to recover from dips in the market. On the other hand, if you're saving for something in the medium term, such as a house deposit, you may want to take less risk

- **Personal attitude** – We all hate the possibility of losing money. In fact, behavioural economists have found that the pain of losing is psychologically about twice as powerful as the pleasure of gaining. However, each of us has our own tolerance to risk. When you're exploring possible investments, it's worth looking at how the investment has performed in the past. As an example, the table below shows how a low-, medium- and high-risk fund have performed in their best and worst years. Looking at each of the worst years, ask yourself how you would feel if your investments fell by such an amount. Would you lose your cool and panic sell? Or hold tight, and maybe even see the dip as an opportunity to invest more?

STILL PANICKING?! Remember, there is a way of investing which doesn't involve selecting your own asset allocation – we'll get to this on pp. 210–12.

	Portfolio composition	Best year return	Worst year fall	Worst 12 months
Low-risk	100% Gilts (British Government Bonds)	1998 +11.4%	2013 -0.8%	-0.9
Medium-risk	50% Gilts, 50% Equities	1997 +18.6%	2008 -8.3%	-14.5%
High-risk	100% Equities	1999 +30.1%	2002 -26.0%	-31.1%

Whatever your attitude to risk, this will determine your asset allocation – the proportion of stocks to bonds in your portfolio. For those wanting to take a slow and steady approach, your portfolio will typically have more funds with government and corporate bonds, while someone with a more ambitious or long-term strategy would hold more shares invested across different sectors and different countries.

Where should I invest?

Now you 'get' investing, you can decide who you're going to trust with your money. Whatever option you choose, it's important that you completely trust your provider and don't feel intimidated. Understanding what you've invested in is so important, so make sure you've done your research and have chosen a method that feels right for you.

For the beginner or nervous investor...

If you've read this chapter and the idea of getting your head around a fund factsheet fills you with dread, then Option 1 or Option 2 might be a safe bet.

Option 1 – Robo-advisors

What are they?
Robo-advisors are just one of the brilliant financial innovations to have emerged over the last decade. You've probably seen them advertised as simple online platforms that take the confusion and time out of investing. For investing newbies, they can be a good choice; usually requiring little to no money to get started and there's no need to worry about the proportion of shares to bonds, as they take care of asset allocation. Think of them as your own robotic personal shopper. Through a brief online survey, you tell them what you like and they'll use clever algorithms to understand your financial goals and work out your asset allocation based on the risk you're willing to take. They'll then invest your money on your behalf, putting it into a variety of ETFs that suit your risk profile.

How to do it

There are now quite a few robo-advisors on the market, each with a slightly different offering. Some might have an 'investment minimum' meaning you need a certain amount of money before you can invest. This is usually fairly low, and almost certainly lower than the minimums you'll come across with a mutual trust fund. Setting up an account is pretty intuitive. Make sure, as always, you understand the fee structure before investing. If you need help thinking about how much risk you're willing to take, go back to pp. 207–9.

Option 2 – Independent financial advisor (IFA)

What is it?

For some, the old-school approach of seeking face to face advice might suit. IFAs are qualified financial planning professionals who give objective advice on making financial decisions and choosing financial products that are best suited to you. IFAs are very useful for people with more complex financial lives. They also help with things such as setting up and transferring pensions or tax planning.

How to do it

Make sure you find an IFA with the appropriate qualifications to ensure they are regulated. Online reviews and asking for recommendations from friends and family is the way to go. Typically, IFAs charge either a percentage fee of the money you want to receive advice on or have managed, a fixed fee for a specific project you would like help with or an hourly charge. (The average UK rate is £150 per hour.) On top of this, you will still pay fees for any investments that they make on your behalf. As you might expect, IFAs tend to be the priciest investment option but may be necessary depending on your needs.

For the confident novice or advanced investor...

If you've read this chapter and got your head around the 'GFY +' sections, then you could consider picking your own funds.

Option 3 – DIY investing

What is it?

For those who want a little more control over their cash and where it goes, you could Nick Knowles it, and build a DIY portfolio. Rather than the personal shopping experience of a robo-advisor, the DIY strategy is like online shopping. Hell you wouldn't dare let a stranger choose what you wear, so you're hardly going to let them invest your hard-earned cash. With this option, you decide how much risk you're willing to take and choose the funds that you want to invest in. If you choose to invest in ETFs, the fees will likely be cheaper than using a robo-advisor. For some, the freedom to choose where their money goes really appeals: you could choose to invest specifically in an ethical fund or one that is actively managed or even buy shares in a specific company. However, whilst you do get additional flexibility, this option puts you in charge of your asset allocation. So, unless you choose a 'balanced fund', also known as a 'hybrid fund' (which contains a mixture of shares and bonds), you have to make the call as to the kinds of funds you invest in and the proportion of shares to bonds.

How to do it

To start your own DIY portfolio, you need to register with a 'fund supermarket' or 'broker', which offers access to lots of funds from different providers. Most fund supermarkets will have tools and resources to help direct you to specific funds. Once you've chosen your platform you can start researching the kinds of funds you want to invest in.

Investing principle 5: Mind the fees

One of the big things to look out for when trying to decide on how you're going to invest and which service you're going to use is the fees. If you're not careful, swathes of your investment could get chomped up. Of course, there are always trade-offs at play; for example, you might be willing to pay a bit more for convenience. The important thing is that you understand what you are being charged and why. The main ones to look out for are:

- **Investment management / platform fees** – A fee that you pay to the fund manager or investment platform
- **Selling/buying funds** – This is usually a flat fee which you pay on buying or selling a fund or shares
- **Transfer out fee** – If you hold an ISA or pension with one platform and move it out to another, it's likely that you'll pay a transfer out fee

How much should I invest?

Once you've selected who you want to invest with, and the kind of risks you're willing to take, you can now think about how much you want to invest.

If you've followed Steps 1 to 5 of the GFY Money Plan then you should have already boosted your emergency savings fund and hopefully be in the habit of squirrelling away a percentage of your post-tax income into a savings account. Now, instead of diverting your percentage into your savings account, you can direct some or all of it into your investment account. How much you invest is up to you but a rule of thumb is to start by thinking about what you can afford to lose. One of the reasons for Grace's investing success was that she only invested money that she could lose. If everything went wrong, it wouldn't affect her lifestyle. She slowly grew her investments over time, spreading the risk. Richard however, did the opposite.

There are two strategies to pick from:

The drip feed strategy – Regularly diverting a set amount of money into your investments each month.

Pros

- Takes advantage of 'pound cost averaging', which means that by making small regular payments you smooth out the highs and lows of the stock market
- Avoids the perils of trying to 'time the market' (see p. 191) and gets you investing ASAP

Cons

- Some investment providers, particularly if you're a DIY investor, have investment minimums, which means you may have to build up a lump sum before investing
- If you're a DIY investor, you'll probably may be charged a fee per transaction

The lump sum strategy – An alternative to the drip feed strategy where you invest a lump sum of money all in one go. If at some point you receive a windfall of cash, this can be a good option.

Pros

- Having the whole sum invested from day one could mean you benefit more from any potential rises in the markets

Cons

- Conversely, having the whole sum invested from day one means you are more exposed to falls in the market

Investing principle 6: Think tax

In this world nothing can be said to be certain, except death and taxes.

Benjamin Franklin

Investments aren't immune to tax either. If you decide to cash in your investments, you *might* have to pay tax. However, depending on the country you live in, it's likely that there will be schemes and allowances that will help to protect some of your money. In the UK, there are a number of 'allowances' that protect investments and savings from tax.

When it comes to investing in stocks and shares, the tax you really need to know about is Capital Gains Tax (CGT). A capital gain is any money you make on investments and is only paid when you come to sell. For example, if you buy shares at £1,000 and then sell them for £1,500, you've made a £500 gain.

CGT is paid on:

- Most personal possessions worth £6,000 or more, apart from your car
- Property that's not your main home
- Your main home if you've let it out, used it for business or if it's very large
- Shares that are not in an ISA
- Business assets

Remember, CGT has nothing to do with your income or salary. The CGT allowance means you can take a certain amount of gains per year before you're charged any tax.

Other types of savings and investments might also be subject to income tax. Dividends, for example, have their own allowance, as well as interest on bonds, bank account savings, corporate bonds and government bonds, which fall into the 'Personal Savings Allowance'. Check HMRC's website to find up-to-date information on allowances.

A great way to permanently protect both your cash savings and investments from tax is through an ISA: a tax-free savings or investment account. Think of an ISA like a piggybank given to you by the government every year. The ISA allowance changes (in the UK the limit is currently £20,000), but, as long as your money is in the piggybank, any interest or gains you make will never be subject to tax.

There are lots of different ISAs and if you want you can pick 'n' mix them, opening more than one kind each year and splitting your allowance between them. The only rule is that you don't exceed the annual allowance.

When it comes to investing in the stock market, there are two to choose from: a Stocks and Shares ISA or a Stocks and Shares Lifetime ISA (LISA). These are a special kind of savings account that don't just hold your money and pay out a set interest rate or bonus (like cash ISAs). Instead they give you the opportunity to invest your money in stocks and shares. This doesn't change how much or little control you have over your investments, you can still use any of the three provider options outlined on pp. 210–12. ISAs are just a vehicle that you use to invest your money, with most investment providers offering them.

TYPES OF ISAS

TYPE		THE DETAIL
STOCKS AND SHARES ISAs invested in stocks and shares	Stocks and Shares ISA	• An investment account that lets you put money into a range of different investments
	Stocks and Shares Lifetime ISA	• An investment account that lets you put money into a range of different investments • Applies the same rules as the Lifetime ISA (see below)
	Junior Stocks and Shares ISA	• For under-eighteens
CASH ISA ISAs that hold your money in cash	Cash ISA	• Offers a set interest rate on your savings • Accessibility varies from fixed rate (where your money is locked in) to easy access
	Lifetime ISA	• For eighteen- to thirty-nine-year-olds • Save up to £4,000 each tax year, every year until your fiftieth birthday • Government will pay an annual bonus of 25 per cent (capped at £1,000 per year) • Use towards first home worth up to £450,000 or at retirement when you've reached sixty • 25 per cent withdrawal charge if not used against a house or at retirement

TYPE		THE DETAIL
	Junior Cash ISA	• Like Cash ISAs for under-eighteens • Set interest rate on savings
INNOVATIVE FINANCE ISA ISAs that hold your money in alternative financial products	An Innovative Finance ISA	• Money held in peer-to-peer lending or crowdfunding products

Another reason you should love ISAs is that you get to open a new one(s) each year. There are tales of 'ISA millionaires' – diligent savers who have religiously opened and maxed out an ISA every year. You can open one of each type and choose to split your ISA allowance. For instance, you might want to hold £1,000 in an easy access Cash ISA and £1,000 in a Stocks and Shares ISA. The only rule is that you have to stay within the annual allowance.

Ethical investing

Recent years have seen huge shifts in our social conscience and the sustainability of our life decisions. So, where, and in what you invest might also be something to think about. A disadvantage of investing in traditional funds is that you, as the investor, have no say over the companies that the fund is invested in. This means that, in theory, you may be investing in a company whose practices do not meet your own principles around sustainability or ethics. Increasingly, however, investment firms have begun to develop new funds that incorporate environmental, social and governance (ESG) factors into their investment strategy. This is often referred to as Socially Responsible Investing (SRI). There are three main ways that funds achieve this:

- **Negative screening** – This means excluding companies because of their involvement in particular areas. For example, a fund might choose to exclude tobacco companies or arms manufacturers
- **Environmental, social and governance (ESG) investing** – This means actively searching for and including companies that meet the fund's ESG criteria. For example, looking for companies that specialize in renewable energy, climate change solutions or gender diverse companies. Some fund managers will go beyond simply using the ESG factors in their search for companies and will try to influence senior management or execute their shareholder voting power to improve ESG practices
- **Impact investing** – In this case, the investment goal is to generate a positive and measurable impact on society and the earth in addition to achieving a financial return

If investing ethically is important to you, look for robo-advisors, funds or IFAs which offer this.

What next?

Invest with your eyes shut

On 19 October 1987 global stock markets had a freak out, marked by a contagion of selling that produced the greatest crash in living memory. 'Black Monday', as it became known, saw the S&P 500 Index lose over 20 per cent in one day. To put that into perspective, imagine investing £10,000 today, only to find it worth less than £8,000 tomorrow. Not cool. It would be tempting to cut your losses and sell, right? But stock markets recover. By the end of the year, the market had gained back all of the loss and ended 2 per cent up for the year. By January 1990, the Dow Jones Index was 60 per cent higher than the Black Monday low. If you'd invested £1,000 in the S&P 500 Index at the close of Black Monday and reinvested your dividends, your portfolio would have been worth a whopping £10,800 twenty years later.

The trouble is, whilst 'buying low and selling high' sounds simple in theory, we're inherently loss averse. When faced with the prospect of losing money, there is an overwhelming urge to pull the plug and scuttle back to the security of your 1.5 per cent savings account. The trick of really successful investing isn't about what you invest in, or when, it's how you deal with the emotional turbulence that goes with the game. You'll never succeed in buying from the very last seller and selling to the very last buyer, so let's focus instead on the time in the market.

Timing the market is a fool's game, whereas time in the market is your greatest natural advantage.

Nick Murray

Remember the story of Grace Groner? She wasn't checking her investments on a day by day basis, panicking at 2 per cent or even 20 per cent falls in the market. The secret to her success was that she closed her eyes and carried on living. So long as your investments are in line with your goals, and you're taking the right kind of risk, you can do the same. Highs and lows are inevitable, but you haven't lost money until you sell.

DO THIS NOW > MAKE IT OFFICIAL

To make sticking to your investment guns even easier, make your investment strategy official. Write down your goals, timeline, asset allocation and risk level.
My investment strategy:

- **Goals** (What are you doing this for?)
- **Timeline** (How long are you investing for?)
- **Asset allocation** (If you're a DIY investor)
- **Or, risk level** (If you're using a robo-advisor/IFA)
- **Charges** (what is the breakdown?)

GFY + REVIEWING YOUR PORTFOLIO

- **Day to day** – Nothing! Stop checking that account
- **Week to week** – I said, stop looking...
- **Month to month** – Seriously? OK, ONE look. But no touching. What were your goals again?
- **Year to year** – One year down! Congrats. OK, now it's time for an annual review...

A good time to review a portfolio is the end of the tax year, when you might be thinking about opening a new ISA. Even if your portfolio has dipped, keep an eye on your long-term goals and hang on in there. The best long-term investors stay invested even when it's scary AF. If you need a gentle reminder as to why this is so important, recap on pp. 189–93. That being said, don't ignore your investments; review your asset allocation or risk level.

To review your portfolio, here are the questions you need to ask yourself:

1. Do you need to rebalance?
- Over the course of a year, your investments are bound to have changed in value, which means that your asset allocation might be out of whack. For example, let's say you originally decided to hold 60 per cent in shares and over the year shares did really well and are now worth 70 per cent of your portfolio. If you've gone down the DIY investor route and chosen your own asset allocation strategy, then you'll have to do this manually: selling or buying more assets to rebalance

your portfolio. If you're investing with a robo-advisor, then all this will be taken care of for you.

2. Have your goals changed?

- Sometimes the unpredictable happens, which might throw a spanner in your perfectly planned investment strategy. For example, perhaps you've inherited some money which means you could buy a property sooner or you've decided to leave your job and take a significant pay cut. Either way, this might mean you're willing to take more or less risk.

- If a change in goals means that you're willing to take less risk, then consider lowering the proportion of stocks to bonds or updating your robo-advisor to invest at a lower level of risk.

3. Are your goals now less than five years away?

- Let's say you were saving for a house deposit and were on track to buy in six years. Two years have passed and you've made 20 per cent on your investments. Because your time horizon is now less than five years, you might want to lower the proportion of shares in your portfolio, perhaps even reduce them to zero. If you've gone down the DIY investor route and chosen your own asset allocation strategy, then you'll have to do this yourself by selling the shares to raise cash or switching to cash equivalents such as low-risk government bonds. However, if you're using a robo-advisor or IFA then it's simply a question of tweaking your risk level or selling some of your investments.

PART 2:

GETTING ON THE PROPERTY LADDER

A letter to aspiring homeowners:

Dear aspiring homeowner,

I wanted to tell you that I'm sorry.

Firstly, you should know that it's not you. It wasn't the matcha lattes or Deliveroos that ate your house deposit away. There was no amount of 'micro-saving' or sifting through the Tesco clearance bin on a Sunday evening that could have fixed this. You see, the real problem is me. I'm f****d.

If the timing were different, maybe this could have worked. Born between 1965 and 1980 and there'd be an 80 per cent chance you'd have bought before thirty. The odds are half that now, and there's a 30 per cent chance you'll be renting for your whole life.

I know this is what you've always wanted: you've been brought up in a culture that puts owning a house on a pedestal and where renting is depressing at best. Remember the rat in the box of cereal? Or the eight-person house share with one bathroom and a shaman flat mate? Those were dark times.

But you deserve better than this. You deserve a system that means having your own place isn't a right for the privileged and an impossibility for those without. One that doesn't just make owning more achievable but renting fairer too. You're not asking for the impossible. Look at Germany,

where longer tenancies and rent controls mean rent is just 23
per cent of net pay, or Paris, where rent caps peg rent to the
median income. It's been done before: historically the UK
has introduced some of the world's most inventive housing
schemes, from Bourneville to the Barbican Estate.

The truth is, you need attention that I can't give you; you
need a government that cares about its renters just as it does
its homeowners, and introduces policies that curb rising
rents, not fuels them further (perhaps ambitious when 19.4
per cent of MPs are also private landlords).

Whilst things might seem bleak for now, know that you've
never been less alone. Things have to change, for you and five
million others.

Not yours,

The housing market

Can I buy?

Unless you're in the very fortunate position of being able to buy
a property in cash, getting one boils down to one thing: can
you borrow money? In home ownership speak, borrowing is
taking out a mortgage: money a bank lends you, which you pay
back over a set period of time (around 25 years), with interest.
Once upon a time, so much as walk past a bank and you'd be
wooed into home ownership, but, post-2008 crisis, things have
tightened up significantly. Banks are both stricter on how much
they'll lend you and the size of deposit required.

For a standard mortgage, you'll need a deposit: the recommended minimum deposit size is 20 per cent of the cost of your home. You can get mortgages with a smaller percentage (as little as 5 per cent), but they'll cost you more in interest. The ratio between the value of your mortgage and the value of your home is called the LTV ratio, with a lower LTV ratio resulting in better mortgage rates.

LOAN TO VALUE RATIOS EXPLAINED

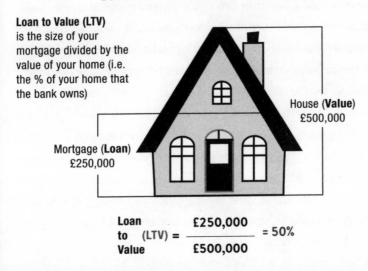

Loan to Value (LTV) is the size of your mortgage divided by the value of your home (i.e. the % of your home that the bank owns)

House (**Value**) £500,000

Mortgage (**Loan**) £250,000

$$\text{Loan to Value (LTV)} = \frac{£250,000}{£500,000} = 50\%$$

As a rule of thumb, you can borrow up to 4.5 times your income. Let's say you and your partner are earning a combined income of £65,000; this means you'd be able to borrow up to £292,500. If you were looking to buy a flat that costs £310,000, then you would need a £17,500 deposit, which would meet the 5 per cent requirement. It is worth noting that saving more than 5 per cent lowers your LTV, giving you access to mortgages with lower interest.

Why are you doing this?

Just because you can buy, doesn't mean you have to. A bit like how puppies aren't just for Christmas, a property isn't either. Houses require money and time to maintain, and selling them isn't cheap. Whilst rental contracts tie you up for months, with a mortgage you're talking years. Don't give in to the societal view of home ownership being the golden gates to adulthood. Renting can mean freedom and, in some cases, more disposable income. If you're thinking about buying with someone, particularly a partner, actually THINK about it. With a rental you can make a swift and easy escape. Own together? Not so much. Question why it is that you're so keen to own. If you've done the sums and you're confident that you can afford it long term, then buying is probably a great option. On the other hand, if there are considerable elements of uncertainty in your life, you're planning on switching jobs, going travelling or starting a business, then leave it until you know your income is secure and you've got your sh*t together(-ish). Not owning is better than getting repossessed.

The GFY guide to getting on the property ladder

If you think buying a property might be on the cards, here's your step by step guide on how to go from home ownership dreams to reality in just eight steps.

☛ = action point

1. Plan

Buying a house doesn't just happen overnight and it can be a long and painful process.

☞ Use a mortgage calculator to work out what you might be able to afford and your target deposit

☞ Decide whether you might use a home-buyer scheme:

- Affordable housing schemes
- Help to Buy equity loan (not to be confused with Help To Buy ISA)
- Shared ownership

☞ Start keeping and organizing your household bills, payslips and outgoings which you'll need as proof of income and expenditure

☞ Check your credit rating and, if necessary, do what you can to improve it (see gofundyourself.co)

☞ If you're self-employed, it's likely you'll need at least two years of accounting records. It's worth seeking advice from a specialist mortgage broker who can help you get things in place

2. Save for a deposit

If you've saved up a deposit – congrats! If not, now's the time to put your budget into action and start saving towards your target deposit.

☞ Set up a budget with a target goal and specific timeframe (see pp. 152–60)

☞ Think about how you could accelerate your saving with a 'savings boost':

- Move in with family or reduce your rent
- Cut back on your wants budget
- Work overtime or get creative about earning some extra income

3. Budget

☞ Budget for home buying expenses

Buying a property comes with an array of other unavoidable costs so make sure you've got the savings to pay for the following:

- Solicitor's fees (£850–£1,500)
- Survey costs (£250–£600)
- Removal costs (£300–£600)
- Buildings insurance (depends on property)
- Initial furnishing and decorating costs (£1,000 +)
- Mortgage arrangement and valuation fees (£150–£1,500)
- Stamp Duty (Land and Buildings Transaction Tax in Scotland, or Land Transaction Tax in Wales)

4. Get mortgage savvy

☞ Decide on a mortgage
☞ Consider a guarantor mortgage where a parent or family member pledges their home or savings as security on your mortgage

There are a variety of mortgages to choose from and understanding the difference can be confusing. However, what you need to know is that there are two main types:

- Fixed rate mortgages: interest rate stays the same for a number of years, regardless of how interest rates change
- Variable rate mortgages: the interest rate can change.

There are advantages and disadvantages to each, and your mortgage provider will be able to advise you on which might be best for you. The GFY + table below should help you to get familiar with the intricacies of each.

GFY + MORTGAGE TYPES

Fixed rate mortgages

The interest rate you pay will stay the same throughout the length of the deal no matter what happens to interest rates. You'll see them advertised as 'two-year fixed rate' or 'five-year fixed rate', for example, along with the interest rate charged for that period

Advantages:

- Peace of mind that your monthly payments will stay the same, helping you to budget

Disadvantages:

- Fixed rate deals could end up being higher than a variable rate mortgage but this will depend on the interest rate
- If interest rates fall, you won't benefit

Watch out for:

- Charges if you want to leave the deal early – you are tied in for the length of the fix

- The end of the fixed period – you should look for
  a new mortgage deal two to three months before
  it ends or you'll be moved automatically onto your
  lender's standard variable rate, which is usually higher

Variable rate mortgages

With variable rate mortgages, the interest rate can change
at any time. Make sure you have some savings set aside so
that you can afford an increase in your payments if rates
do rise.

Variable rate mortgages come in various forms:

Type	Advantages	Disadvantages
Standard variable rate (SVR) This is the normal interest rate your mortgage lender charges homebuyers and it will last as long as your mortgage or until you take out another mortgage deal. Changes in the interest rate might occur after a rise or fall in the base rate set by the Bank of England.	• Freedom – you can overpay or leave at any time	• Your rate can be changed at any time during the loan

Type	Advantages	Disadvantages
Discount mortgages This is a discount on the lender's standard variable rate (SVR) and only applies for a certain length of time, typically two or three years. But it pays to shop around. SVRs differ across lenders, so don't assume that the bigger the discount, the lower the interest rate. **Example** Two banks have discount rates: • Bank A has a 2 per cent discount off a SVR of 6 per cent (so you'll pay 4 per cent) • Bank B has a 1.5 per cent discount off a SVR of 5 per cent (so you'll pay 3.5 per cent) Though the discount is larger for Bank A, Bank B will be the cheaper option.	• Cost – the rate starts off cheaper, which will keep monthly repayments lower • If the lender cuts its SVR, you'll pay less each month	• Budgeting – the lender is free to raise its SVR at any time • If the Bank of England base rates rise, you'll probably see the discount rate increase too Watch out for: • Charges if you want to leave before the end of the discount period

Type	Advantages	Disadvantages
Tracker mortgages Tracker mortgages move directly in line with another interest rate – normally the Bank of England's base rate plus a few per cent. If the base rate goes up by 0.5 per cent your rate will go up by the same amount. Usually they have a short life, typically two to five years, though some lenders offer trackers that last for the life of your mortgage or until you switch to another deal.	• If the rate it is tracking falls, so will your mortgage payments	• If the rate it is tracking increases, so will your mortgage payments • You might have to pay an early repayment charge if you want to switch before the deal ends Watch out for • The small print – check your lender can't increase rates even when the rate your mortgage is linked to hasn't moved. It's rare, but it has happened in the past
Capped rate mortgages Your rate moves in line normally with the lender's SVR. But the cap means the rate can't rise above a certain level.	• Certainty – your rate won't rise above a certain level. But make sure you can afford repayments if it rises to the level of the cap • Cheaper – your rate will fall if the SVR comes down	• The cap tends to be set quite high • The rate is generally higher than other variable and fixed rates • Your lender can change the rate at any time up to the level of the cap

Type	Advantages	Disadvantages
Offset mortgages These work by linking your savings and current account to your mortgage so that you only pay interest on the difference. You still repay your mortgage every month as usual, but your savings act as an overpayment that helps to clear your mortgage early. **Example** If you've a mortgage of £150,000 and savings of £15,000, then you only pay interest on the difference of £135,000.	• You are able to overpay your mortgage each month so you could be mortgage-free sooner • You can reduce your monthly payments • Can be tax efficient as you won't pay tax on savings income – good for higher rate taxpayers	• The rate is generally higher than standard mortgages • You won't earn interest on your savings and/or current account

© Money Advice Service

5. Get advice and compare deals

☛ Use the following sources to find the best deal **for you**

- **Search online** – compare deals across a number of providers
- **Mortgage brokers** – typically provide a more personal service and guidance
- **Your bank** – might provide a better deal for existing customers

All banks and brokers must offer advice when they recommend a mortgage. You can choose your own mortgage without seeking advice, which is called an 'execution-only' application. However, this comes with the risk of not choosing a mortgage that is right for your situation or being rejected by the mortgage provider because you weren't familiar with the requirements and restrictions.

Also, whilst shopping around remember to look at the fees, as well as the exit penalties (paid when your balance is cleared early or when you switch to a new lender).

☛ Get an 'agreement in principle' from your mortgage provider

Once you've chosen a mortgage provider and taken advice on the kind of mortgage that would be right for you, apply for what is called an 'agreement in principle'. This will mean that any offers you make are more likely to be accepted and will make the process smoother.

6. Make an offer

The fun part – actually finding that home you've been dreaming about. Compromise is inevitable so make sure you've set apart your 'must haves' from your 'nice to haves'.

☛ Find the place you want and put in an offer

7. Secure your mortgage and carry out surveys

☛ Formally apply for a mortgage

☛ Appoint a property solicitor (also known as a conveyancer) to carry out surveys and manage the legal side of the purchase

☛ Agree to the terms of the sale

8. Finalize

Your mortgage will now be approved (hopefully) and your lender may ask you to insure the property as part of the approval process.

☛ Put down your deposit

☛ Exchange contracts. This means you are locked into a legally binding deal to buy the house or flat

☛ Organise the move – book removal company, cleaners, etc.

☛ Pick up your keys! On completion day, you'll be able to pick up the keys from the estate agent or seller

☛ Pop some bottles…

Live and give

If you've completed steps 1 to 6, firstly, congratulations! Secondly, you're probably wondering: now what? You've paid off bad debts, got yourself a boosted emergency fund, sorted your pension and you're officially an investor. In terms of financial goals, you've smashed it.

So now what? You didn't get this far for the sheer joy of watching your debts shrink and the figures in your investment account climb. You had an idea in mind, a reason for reading nearly 60,000 words on personal finance! I said from the start that this book isn't a guide to getting loaded or retiring before forty. Instead, it's about how you can earn, spend and invest your way towards living your best life and maybe even help others live their best lives too. Be it donating money, investing your time in someone, treating a friend or maybe even a stranger, the effects of giving are powerful.

> *We make a living by what we get, but we make a life by what we give.*
>
>   Winston Churchill

But if you've taken one thing away from this book I hope it's that being 'good at money' isn't just about opening an ISA or starting to budget. That's the easy bit. Instead, it's about the bigger picture: How can you feel excited to spend rather than guilty because it's money you don't have? And how can you earn it in a sustainable way that doesn't leave you loathing every working hour?

I hope that *Go Fund Yourself* has got you thinking about the big questions because, at the end of the day, we only have one life so let's spend it wisely.

Acknowledgements

I owe a huge thank you to the people who believed this book to be worthwhile and who made it happen.

Firstly, to my publisher Head of Zeus and in particular to my brilliant, and ever calm, editor Ellen, for having faith in my idea, making it a reality and for her guidance along the way. Also a big thanks to Clémence, Jessie and the design team for bringing the book to life so beautifully and to Chrissy, my supremely talented, ever supportive friend and (actual) lifesaver, without whom this book wouldn't have happened.

To my supportive friends. To Graham for your accountancy expertise and support, Toby for your brutal honesty and reassurance that this book 'is actually alright' and to Chris for coming up with such a brilliant title. Pravina, Charlotte, Sarah and Torie, thank you for not thinking (or at least not telling me) that I was completely mad to write this and for your feedback along the way.

Thank you also to Jonathon for your investing wisdom, Ebi for always listening and believing and to Coffee, Geek and Friends for allowing me to take up residence for most of 2018, and for the best banana bread and coffee in London.

And, of course, last but by no means least, the biggest thank you to my parents. Thank you for always encouraging me to take risks and for teaching me that there is more to life than the bottom line. Love you.

Alice x

Resources

Beyond the Book

Go Fund Yourself isn't just a book, it's also an online platform and community!

www.gofundyourself.co contains loads of resources and tools which take the boring out of finance.

You can also find me on Instagram @go_fund_yourself_

Index